CENTERING BLACK NARRATIVE

First published in 2016 by Itrah Press

© Copyright Itrah Press 2016
ISBN 978-0-9982781-9-3

Editor: Tariq al-Amin
Typesetting & cover art by Etherea Design

Printed and bound in the United States

Contents

Dedication

For Adam, Zayd, Aaliyah, Nasir, Nyeem and Ajaha.

﴿وَنُرِيدُ أَن نَّمُنَّ عَلَى الَّذِينَ اسْتُضْعِفُوا فِي الْأَرْضِ وَنَجْعَلَهُمْ أَئِمَّةً وَنَجْعَلَهُمُ الْوَارِثِينَ﴾

And We wanted to bestow favor on those who were deemed weak and oppressed in the land, and make them leaders and inheritors.
(Qur'an 28:5)

CENTERING BLACK NARRATIVE

*Black Muslim Nobles Among
the Early Pious Muslims*

co-authored by
Ahmad Mubarak &
Dawud Walid

ITRAH PRESS
PUBLISHING

Foreword
Introduction to
Arabs and Blackness

Ustadh Abdullah bin Hamid Ali

W.E.B. Dubois famously said that "...the problem of the twenti-
eth century is the problem of the color line."[1] It appears that the
color line is also the problem of the twenty first century. When
it comes to the question of the value of "black" lives, it seems
that more important than color, "blackness" has been a problem
of practically every century of recorded history. While it is very
easy to trace the origins of color-based race stratification, in all
major civilizations there is evidence of a disdain for dark-er skin
and the subsequent denial of the same social privilege given to
those of lighter skin. This is true of the ancient Chinese where
northerners practiced color discrimination against the darker
skinned inhabitants of the south; the Brahmans of India who
discriminated against their darker Dravidian counterparts; and
it even appears to have been the case in Arabia, especially with

---

1   W.E.B. Dubois introduces his "Forethought" from *The Souls of Black Folks*
with the following:

> "Herein lie buried many things which if read with patience, may
> show the strange meaning of being black here at the dawning of
> the Twentieth century. This meaning is not without interest to you,
> Gentle Reader; for the problem of the Twentieth century is the prob-
> lem of the color line."

W.E.B. Dubois. *The Souls of Black Folks*. New York: Simon and Schuster Paperbacks, 2009 edition, p. 3

regard to indigenous Africans both before and upon the passing of the Prophet Muhammad. Besides the obvious disparities in political, economic, military, and cultural capital between whites and others, white supremacy and black antipathy find meaning socially through the sale of skin whitening creams. In India where whitening creams are used by both women and men, sales are in excess of a 300 million dollar per year industry, vastly outpacing sales of Coca Cola.[2] Even in African countries like Nigeria, according to the World Health Organization, up to 77% of Nigerian women utilize skin whitening creams.[3] Practically, every language, including those of Africa, contains metaphors of white positivity and black negativity. And according to the South African scholar, David Goldenberg, the Hamitic myth relegating black Africans to perpetual slavery to non-blacks spread amongst Muslims in the 7th century during Arab incursions into North Africa, not only during the transatlantic slave trade. According to Goldenberg,

> Beginning with the fourth-century Syriac Christian *Cave of Treasures*, a biblical tradition that saw Canaan as cursed with slavery now included a statement informing the reader or listener that Canaan was the ancestor of dark-skinned people. The link of blackness and slavery in the various versions of the work is clear, though implicit, while an explicit link, in the form of a dual curse of both blackness and slavery, begins to appear in seventh-century Islamic texts. This exegetical innovation coincides with the seventh-century Muslim conquests in Africa, which brought an increasing influx of black African slaves to the Near East. From this time onward, the Curse of Ham, that is, the exegetical tie between black-

2   Garner, Steve. Racisms: *An Introduction*. London: SAGE Publications Ltd, 2010, p. 79

3   World Health Organization. "Preventing Disease through Healthy Environments: Mercury in Skin Lightening Products." 2011 report. (http://www.who.int/ipcs/assessment/public_health/mercury_flyer.pdf). See also Adow, Mohammed. "Nigeria's Skin Whitening Obsession: Nigeria has the world's highest percentage of women using skin lightening agents in the quest for "beauty."" Al-Jazeera: 6 April 2013. (http://www.aljazeera.com/indepth/features/2013/04/20134514845907984.html)

ness and servitude, is commonly found in works composed in the Near East, whether in Arabic by Muslims or in Syriac by Christians. The increasing reliance on the Curse coincides with the increasing numbers of Blacks taken as slaves.[4]

Do black lives matter? And what *is* a "black" person? Depending on where and when you ask this question, the answers will surely differ. "Black" in Brazil or Haiti or Morocco or Egypt clearly connotes something different from what it does in the United States of America. If "black" can be proven to be geographically and culturally determined, then can it be said that "blackness" or a "black person" is not a real thing? And would it be legitimate to pose a similar question about "whiteness" or "Arabness"?

Race denotes a number of things, but, for premodern peoples, it was largely determined by shared language, religion, and culture. During the enlightenment period, however, the concept was transformed into a term of stratification denoting genetic homogeneity between varied geographic populations in light of certain shared phenotypic traits like skin color, hair texture, lip size, and nose shape. Additionally, "race" became freighted with political baggage implying innate superiority of some people over and above others resulting from the quadripartite racial division of the 18th century Swedish botanist, Carl Linnaeus (1707-1778). Linnaeus' racial taxonomy promoted both biological and behavioral determinism, like innate (white) optimism, (black) laziness, (yellow) dejection, or (red) savagery. In terms of motivations, each person was believed to act according to his/her appetite (blacks), habit (reds), beliefs (yellows), or rationality (whites).

Pace the 19th century, an even more sinister idea was introduced by the French aristocrat Arthur De Gobineau (1816-1882), pioneer of the Aryan Master Race theory. According to Gobineau, civilization being the pinnacle of evolutionary socio-cultural advancement, could only and ever exist to the extent that a group of people possess some degree of Aryan blood. In other words, if any civilization has ever existed, it was only due to the presence of

---

4   David M. Goldenberg. *The Curse of Ham: Race and Slavery in Judaism, Christianity, and Islam*. Princeton and Oxford: Princeton University Press, 2003, p. 197

Aryan blood running in their veins. On the other hand, the lower the admixture of Aryan blood, the more likely socio-political and cultural degeneration would become an eventuality. Gobineau says, after enumerating ten historical civilizations (the Indians, Egyptians, Assyrians, Greeks, Chinese, Italians, the Germanic tribes, Alleghenians, Mexicans, and Peruvians),

> In the above list, no negro race is seen as the initiator of a civilization. Only when it is mixed with some other can it even be initiated into one. Similarly, no spontaneous civilization is to be found among the yellow races; and when the Aryan blood is exhausted stagnation supervenes.[5]

In this same century, whites were divided into three subdivisions: 1) Nordic, 2) Alpine, and 3) Mediterranean. In other words, Arabs, being Mediterranean, were officially inducted into the "white" race. Goldenberg says,

> The Arab conquests also had another consequence. Where skin color in Arabic literature previously described personal complexion, it is now used to designate ethnic groups, with "black" referring to the dark-skinned peoples. The same phenomenon occurred in sixteenth-century England. After England's encounter with black Africans, white and black became the terminology of "self" and "other." Both Arabs and English begin to use color terms as ethnic markers to distinguish others of darker or lighter skin when they discovered such people.[6]

The ease with which race has been and can be transformed reveals, as has already been acknowledged by the scientific community, that race is nothing more than a sociological phenomenon rather than a biological fact. This is not to imply that race is

---

5   Arthur Gobineau, Adrian Collins. *The Inequality of Human Races*, New York: G.P. Putman's Sons. 1915, p. 212.
6   David M. Goldenberg. *The Curse of Ham: Race and Slavery in Judaism, Christianity, and Islam.* Princeton and Oxford: Princeton University Press, 2003, p. 197

not "real." It is to say, rather, that race is in actuality a collective consciousness and sense of solidarity acquired through the experience of one particular group vis-à-vis one or more others. Put another way, race is an "experience" rather than an expression indicative of genetic homogeneity shared in common between certain geographic populations.

For the purpose of this book, these facts are important because without considering them, especially when reading classical religious literature, one can easily misread both the content and context of early writers. Among those writers are many who anathematize Muslims for characterizing the Prophet Muhammad—God's blessing and peace upon him—as black, even though descriptions of Prophet Muhammad are disparate. He is quoted as saying in one sound tradition, "I was sent to the *red* (i.e. white) and the black."[7] In another tradition, he relates to the second caliph Abu Bakr a vision or dream he had saying, "I had a vision of myself being followed by black sheep who were being followed by a flock of white sheep until the black sheep could no longer be seen." Abu Bakr reportedly said, "O God's Messenger! As for the black sheep, they are the Arabs. They will enter Islam and multiply. The white sheep are the non-Arabs. They will enter Islam until the Arabs will be no longer be recognized due to their numerousness." The Prophet reportedly said, "This is precisely the interpretation offered by the Angel [Gabriel] prior to dawn."[8]

In other words, the "black" to whom the Prophet was sent and the "black" sheep overshadowed by the white sheep are the Arabs and other "blacks." Imam Nawawi (1233-1277) clearly has no problem with the validity of such an interpretation.[9] And the

---

7 Yahya b. Sharaf Al-Nawawī. Ṣaḥīḥ Muslim bi Sharh al-Nawawi, Beirut: Dār al-Fikr, 1995, 3:1/4

8 Imam Suyuti relates this hadith from Sa'id b. Mansur via Sa'id b. al-Musayyab and Ibn Abi Layla. Al-Suyuti, 'Abd Abd Al-Rahman Jalal al-Din. Tarikh al-Khulafa'. Cairo: Dar al-Fajr li al-Turath, 2004, p. 86

9 Imam Yaḥyā b. Sharaf al-Nawāwī (676/1278), the famous commentator on the canonical work known as Ṣaḥīḥ Muslim, says of this statement,

> It has been said that the "red" is a reference to the non-Arab whites (al-bīd min al-'ajam), and the "black" refers to the Arabs since brownness (sumra) is predominant among them and the people of the Sudan. It has also been said that the "black" refers to those of the Sudan, while the "red" is a reference to the Arabs and others.

Lebanese scholar Na'um Shaqir (1863-1922) who authored *Tarikh al-Sudan* (History of the Blacks) lists Arabs as a subspecies of blacks in light of these considerations.[10] If this is true, it would seem uncontroversial to call the Prophet "black", since he was, afterall, an Arab. Despite the soundness of this logic, Muslim orthodox teachings have been so as to consider anyone who characterizes the Prophet as "black" to be apostates who are to be executed without delay having no opportunity for redemption.[11]

Rather than arguing that this opinion is flawed or backwards as is the tendency of many modern Muslims, I would contend that it's important to completely consider the context from which those scholars were writing. Firstly, they argue that what is fundamentally problematic about such a characterization is that it attributes to the Prophet—God's blessing and peace upon him—a description by which he was not known. In other words, while there are many different ways the Prophet's color is described in the biographical literature (one report describing him as 'akhdar'... or green as a metaphor for "dark"),[12] none of the traditions describe his as being 'aswad', the standard word for 'black.' So, it is simply a matter of mischaracterizing the Prophet Muham-

---

It has been said as well that the "red" are human beings, and the "black" are the sprites (*jinn*). All of these views are correct, since he was dispatched to all of them.

Yaḥya b. Sharaf Al-Nawawī. *Ṣaḥīḥ Muslim bi Sharḥ al-Nawawi*, Beirut: Dār al-Fikr, 1995, 3:1/4

10   Na'um Shaqir says,

Ethiopia was known both in Egyptian ruins and in the Torah by the name, Kush. Ethiopia is the name the Greeks gave to all the lands of the blacks and those of intensely dark brown skin. It means, "black face" or "burnt." When it is used without qualification, it refers to the lands of the Sudanese, Abyssinians, and the Arabs...

Na'um Shaqir. *Tarikh al-Sudan*. Beirut: Dar al-Jil, 1981, 1/9

11   Qāḍī 'Ayyāḍ Abū al-Faḍl Al-Yaḥsubī. *Al-Shifā bi Ta'rīf Huqūq al-Muṣṭafā*, Beirut: Dār al-Kutub al-'Ilmiya, 2000, pp. 130-183.

12   Fayruzabadi, author of the famed lexicon, *Al-Qamus Al-Muhit*, says, "Green is black" (al-akhdar al-aswad). Fayumi says in *Al-Misbah Al-Munir*, "The Arabs call 'green' 'black' because that's the way it appears from a distance." Fayruzabadi, Muhammad b. Ya'qub. *Al-Qamus Al-Muhit*. Beirut: Dar al-Fikr, 1995, p. 347; Fayumi, Ahmad b. Muhammad. *Al-Misbah Al-Munir*. Beirut: Al-Maktaba Al-'Asriya, 1997, p. 153

mad—God's blessing and peace upon him, which can be taken as a form of disparagement according this view's proponents. The second reason for this view of Muslim theologians is that 'aswad' or black during their age connoted things which were very negative. One could surmise that this was further magnified by the very fact that most of the Arabs became "white," as predicted by the aforementioned prophetic tradition.

Conversely, it could be argued that characterizing Prophet Muhammad as "white" (abyad) is the result of interpretive preponderating (tarjih). That is to say that a *choice* was made according to a certain criteria accepted by many Muslim theologians to prefer hadiths which state or imply that the Prophet was "white-skinned" over other descriptions which suggest otherwise. As a matter of fact, the most widely accepted versions of the Prophet's physical description utilize the somewhat ambiguous wording "azhar al-lawn," which has been interpreted by many scholars as meaning, "white-skinned." Some versions describe him as "white imbued with redness" (abyad mushrab humratan); some say he was like "the pith of a date-palm tree"; others "like an ingot of silver"; "dark" (akhdar); and in Tirmidhi's collection from Anas b. Malik, "brown colored" (asmar al-lawn).[13] According to Hafiz Dhahabi, "Whenever someone is called "white", it means "wheat-colored."[14]

With this much discrepancy, it seems that theologians who anathematized Muslims for merely describing the Prophet as black had no solid basis for this ruling, since the reports of the Prophet's putative "whiteness" is neither the result of indisputably authentic reports (tawatur) nor a matter of religion (din) for which a person can be declared an apostate. Otherwise, the authors of Sunni manuals of orthodox dogmatic theology, like Tahawi, would have included this among the required beliefs of all Muslims. The absence of this point of doctrine further corroborates the claim that belief in the Prophet's putative "whiteness" is *not* a requirement of Muslim faith. Even if true, it can

---

13   See Ibn Hajar al-'Asqalani's attempt to reconcile the conflicting reports in Ahmad b. 'Ali b. Hajar al-'Asqalani. *Fath Al-Bari Sharh Sahih al-Bukhari*, Beirut: Dar al-Manar, 1992, 6/623-624.
14   Al-Dhahabi Muhammad b. Ahmad b. 'Uthman. *Siyar al-A 'lam al-Nubala'*, Beirut: Mu'assasa al-Risala, 1981

be compared to declaring a person to be an apostate for denying the existence of China.

As for scholars who believe that the offense has less to do with the mischaracterization of the Prophet's person but that calling someone "black" is universally disparaging, this would necessitate that there were no "black" prophets and that it would likewise be disparaging to characterize any of them in such terms. We know the first claim is false, because the Qur'an says, *We have sent a messenger to every nation*[15] and *We sent messengers before you. Among them are some whose accounts We have given you and others whose accounts We have not given you.*[16] As for the latter claim, there are a number of sages and prophets who have been described as either black or dark brown, including Luqman, Moses[17] and Jesus.[18] In addition, if "black" is universally dispar-

---

15 Qur'an 16:36

16 Qur'an 40:78

17 Ibn Hishām reports in his *Sīra* concerning the miraculous event known as the Prophet Muḥammad's Night Journey and Ascension to Heavens (*al-Isrā' wa al-Miʿrāj*) that when he reached the sixth heaven he saw "A very dark man (*rajulun ādam*), tall, and hook-nosed resembling the men of Shanū'a. I said to him: Who is this, Gabriel? He replied: "This is your brother, Moses, son of ʿImrān."" ('Abd Al-Malik b. Hishām. *Al-Sīra Al-Nabawiya*, Beirut: Mu'assasa al-Maʿārif, 2004, p. 205).

18 Imam Bukhari reports the following hadith on the authority of the Prophet's companion, Ibn ʿUmar, who reported that the Prophet Muhammad said:

> "While I was asleep, I saw myself circumambulating the Ka'ba, when suddenly there was a man with dark brown skin (adam) and straight hair dripping with water [being supported between two men. I asked: "Who is this?" They responded: "The Son of Mary."

This description of Jesus is contradicted by another hadith reported by both Bukhari and Muslim on the authority of Abu Hurayra who reported that,

> "The Messenger of Allah said: "On the night I was taken on the miraculous journey, I met Moses." He then described him: "He was a slender man with hair that curled at its ends. He resembled one of the men of the Shanu'a tribe." He then said, "I also met Jesus. He was mid-height with white (*ahmar*) skin. He looked as if he had just come out of a bathhouse."

Upon hearing this, the companion, Ibn ʿUmar, objected to hearing others describe Jesus as "white" (*ahmar*),

> "No! By God! The Messenger of Allah did NOT say that Jesus was white (*ahmar*). What he actually said was: "While I was circum-

aging, it would mean that it is unlawful to refer any given person as "black", since the Qur'an says, *Do not speak ill of one another; do not use offensive nicknames for one another.*[19]

According to Jahiz (776-869), the 9th century east African rationalist scholar of the Mu'tazilite sect, all ten of the Prophet's paternal uncles, from his grandfather 'Abdul-Muttalib, were dark brown.20 It would stand to reason, then, that if Prophet Muhammad was not a dark-skinned man, he was definitely the offspring of a tribe of dark brown people. According to linguists like Ibn Manzur, Tha'lab, and other scholars like Ibn Athir and Nawawi, the majority of Arabs were light and dark brown (as-mar wa adam). Were we to classify the early Arabs according to popular taxonomies in western countries today, they would easily fall under the "colored" or "black" designation.

Though the early Arabs considered themselves to be a distinct race from the surrounding populations, they did not characterize themselves as "white." Rather, the "whites" of their day were those of Persia, Byzantium, and the Levant, who they referred to as "the reds" (al-hamra), since "white" was an offensive characterization most commonly used to indicate that a person had unattractive spots of albino-like discoloration on their skin, a condition known today as "vitiligo." For this reason, Ibn Manzūr says in his *Lisān al-'Arab*,

> Red (*aḥmar*) means white (*abyaḍ*); [said as a way of] taking flight from the description of vitiligo (*baraṣ*).[21]

---

ambulating the Ka'ba, I suddenly saw a dark-brown man (*adam*) with straight hair being supported between two men. His head was dripping with water" or "His head was pouring with water. I then said, "Who is this?" They said: "The Son of Mary." I then turned my attention in another direction and noticed a large white (*ahmar*) man, with curly hair, and a bleary right eye which looked like a protruding grape. I asked, "Who is this?" They said: "The anti-Christ (*Dajjal*)." The one he resembles the most is Ibn Qatan."

19   Qur'an 49:12

20   *Rasa'il al-Jahiz*. (Abd Al-Salam Muhammad Harun Edition). Cairo: Maktaba al-Khaniji, 1964, p. 209

21   Ibn Manẓūr, Muḥammad b. Mukrim al-Afrīqī al-Miṣrī. *Lisān al-'Arab*, Beirut: Dār Ṣādir, 1882, p. 209

When not used disapprovingly, "white" was used as a laudable quality of human character according to Arabic lexicographers. The famed Arabic linguist, Tha'lab of Kūfa, was asked, "Why has the word "red" (*aḥmar*) been given special treatment as opposed to the word "white" (*abyaḍ*)?" He said,

> Because the Arabs don't say that someone is white due to the whiteness of their skin. Rather, the one they consider to be white is the one who is pure and free of defects. So whenever they mean that someone is white-skinned, they call him red (*aḥmar*).[22]

The fact that "white" during the prophetic era was taken to be disparaging would mean that if "black" is an offensive characterization, "white" would also be offensive *a fortiori*.

As already stated, the Arabs did not describe themselves as a "white" race for more than one reason. They, however, appear to have tolerated being subsumed under the category of the "blacks." For this reason, Jahiz characterizes the Arabs as "quasi-blacks" and Africans as "true blacks."[23] According to this line of reasoning, why would it be acceptable to characterize Prophet Muhammad as "white" but not "black"? In reality, the most appropriate course of action would be to avoid describing him and Arabs as either white or black in light of all the cultural baggage those two terms bear today. He was neither an African nor a European. That is so, even if we incline to subsume him under the category of "white" due to certain reports or "black" in light of others and the fact that most Arabs were a swarthy people of light and dark brown.

One may ask: why is any of this important? Why the "obsession" with race when we know that Allah doesn't judge people on the basis of skin color, and the Prophet condemned racism and race pride? The fact is that although chattel slavery and racial segregation in the world are generally considered things of the past, we still live with the legacy of those oppressive systems. And how could we possibly shake off the residue of centuries

---

22   Muḥammad b. Mukrim b. Manẓūr al-Afrīqī al-Miṣrī. *Lisān al-'Arab*, Beirut: Dār Ṣādir, 1882, p. 209
23   *Rasa'il al-Jahiz*. (Abd Al-Salam Muhammad Harun Edition). Cairo: Maktaba al-Khaniji, 1964, p. 223

of indoctrination into race supremacy and inferiority without a robust and honest discussion of its etiology?

The truth is that contemporary *perceptions* arise from historical *conceptions*. And those perceptions are reinforced every time we watch the news and Hollywood films. We still live with stereotypes of the lazy black criminal parasite and the hard working white success. But, we've added the angry Arab terrorist and conniving Latino drug smuggler.

Pharaoh is portrayed in the Qur'an as the archetypal tyrant. The Qur'an says, *"Verily, Pharaoh exceeded bounds in the earth, stratifying its inhabitants, while oppressing a group therefrom: slaughtering their sons and sparing their womenfolk. Indeed, he was among those who spread corruption."*[24] Pharaoh also declared himself to be God, *"I am your lord, most high."*[25] Then, on the back of his slaves and the help if his military and economic ministers, he constructed a spectacular civilization the glory of which he claimed all credit.

Understanding the elements of Pharaoh's success and that had it not been for divine intervention the Children of Israel would have lived in permanent servitude, it should help us see the importance of undoing the harms of racial stratification and the necessity of reviving an iconoclastic religio-social consciousness. The most salient harms that arise from contemporary racial stratification are two things: one is of a deeply spiritual nature, and the other pertains to the promotion of humanity. The spiritual concern relates to what Dr. Sherman Jackson refers to as white supremacy constituting the beginning of a modern form of idolatry which Muslims and non-Muslims need to show enormous care to resist. When one type of person is conferred with an authority which is reserved only to the creator (e.g. the determination of good and evil, beauty, art, progress), especially without challenging the epistemic bases of those judgments, one is in peril of committing idolatry. On the other hand, when the economic and political elite of any society classifies people in hierarchies from highest to lowest value, especially when not based on objective merit, one has already taken the first step toward the justification of genocide.

---

24   Qur'an 28:4
25   Qur'an 79:24

To ignore the subject of race in our times is tantamount to giving tacit approval to mass murder, inequitable allocation of government resources, incarceration disparities, political over-representation, economic disadvantage, and educational inaccessibility; it justifies shedding tears for the murder of French babies but not those who belong to Iraqi parents; it legitimizes intervention in European genocides but not those happening in Africa; it condones the mistreatment of the victims of police brutality, not the victimizers; it also leads us to conclude first amendment rights belong only to white European faces. Finally, ignoring the uncomfortable subject of race in our times causes us to claim to be living in a post racial world; a world which suddenly surprises us when we find racist demagogues the frontrunners in our national politics.

Centering Black Narrative

What do we mean when we classify the following personalities as "Black"? When one hears the term black one may conjure up a plethora of different images and or ideas. Do we mean black as in a race based definition which is used by social scientists? What is race itself? Is race an immutable physical categorization as claimed by the eugenics movement? Those theories had roots in the now debunked taxonomies of Swedish polymath Carl Linnaeus. (d. 1778) in the tenth edition of his "Systema Naturae", Linnaeus arbitrarily divided humans into different races based on their hues and attributed stereotypical characteristics to such taxonomies based on the classical four temperaments of antiquity. His classifications were so influential that he is called the father of taxomny. Another influential writer on the subject of human taxonomy was the German scientist Johann Friedrich Blumenbach.

Blumenbach on the other hand classified humans arbitrarily according to the shape of their skulls. He wrote a couple of treatises on race taxonomy over the course of his career. Blumenbach's final taxonomy of 1795 divided all humans into five groups, defined both by geography and appearance--in his order, the Caucasian variety, for the light-skinned people of Europe and adjacent parts of Asia and Africa; the Mongolian variety, for most other inhabitants of Asia, including China and Japan; the Ethiopian variety, for the dark- skinned people of Africa; the American variety, for most native populations of the New -the aborigines of Australia. But Blumenbach's original classification of 1775 recognized only the first four of these five, and united members of the Malay variety with the other people of Asia whom Blumenbach came to name Mongolian.[26] Blumenbach states in regards to Caucasians: "Caucasian variety. I have taken the name of this variety from Mount Caucasus, both because its neighborhood, and especially its southern slope, produces the most beautiful race of men, I mean the Georgian; and because ... in that region, if anywhere, it seems we ought with the greatest probability to place the autochthones [original forms] of mankind. That stock displays... the most beautiful form of the skull, from which, as from a mean and primeval type, the others diverge... Besides, it is white in color, which we may further assume to be the primitive color of mankind, since... it is very easy to degenerate into brown, but very much more difficult for dark to become white."[27]

The irony of the travesty which resulted in race base pseudo-science which Blumenbach seems to be the progenitor of, is that he himself expressed that these taxonomies weren't based on capacity or racial superiority or inferiority. For example he states: "Finally, I am of opinion that after all these numerous instances I have brought together of negroes of capacity, it would not be difficult to mention entire well-known provinces of Europe, from out of which you would not easily expect to obtain off-hand such good authors, poets, philosophers, and correspondents of the Paris Academy; and on the other hand, there is no so-called savage nation known under the sun which has so much distinguished itself by such examples of perfectibility and original capacity for scientific culture, and thereby attached itself so closely to the most civilized nations of the earth, as the Negro." He was certainly the most genial of European thinkers of time.

In reality race itself is a social construct that has very little to do with physical traits. An example of this would be the fact that Japanese people were once considered "Honorary Whites" by the racist apartheid regime of South Africa. Tokyo's Yawata Iron and Steel Company offered to purchase 5,000,000 tons of South African pig iron over a 10 year period for the amount of $250,000,000. [28]

---

26   http://discovermagazine.com/1994/nov/thegeometerofrac441
27   Johan Freidrich Blumenbach, *The Anthropological Treatises of Johan Friedrich Blumenbach*, " The Natural Varieties of Mankind", London: The Anthropological Society, 1865, p.265
28   Time, South Africa: Honorary Whites, 19 January 1962

As a result of this trade pact, the South African government which structured its entire society around demarcations of race, bestowed white status upon Japan in exchange for financial gain. Evidently being a part of the superior white race was available to those who could pay for it for those who weren't blessed by providence to have the actual white phenome. The small Chinese community in South Africa at the time also appealed for whiteness. They did so based on 5 markers/arguments:

1. Convince whites that they made a positive virtue based on race distinctiveness.

2. Adjusting their lifestyle to be more acceptable to whites.

3. Constructing parallel institutions.

4. Develop a reputation for academic excellence.

5. Differentiating themselves from blacks.[29]

Their struggle for whiteness was not all in vain as they were granted the same rights as the Japanese in regards to the equal treatment according to the Group Areas Act in 1984.[30] That basically meant that they were not required to use segregated facilities and were exempted from some of the discriminatory laws that applied to some non-Whites. They still couldn't vote etc. Other East Asian nationalities such as Taiwanese and South Koreans were given full honorary white status. South Korea severed ties with South Africa as a result of apartheid in 1978 and didn't resume diplomatic relation until 1992.[31]

Taiwan was also blessed with the high distinction of honorary whiteness by the apartheid government. This was due to Taiwan being South Africa's fifth largest trading partner. Even the Nazi regime of Adolf Hitler bestowed the status of Honorary Aryans upon the Japanese. Hitler's designation of the Japanese as hon-

---

29 Afro-Hispanic Review: White, Honorary White, or Non-White: Apartheid Era Constructions of Chinese, Dr. Yoon Jung Park (Univ of Johannesburg), Spring 2008
30 Masako Osada, *Sanctions and Honorary Whites: Diplomatic Policies and Economic Realities In Relations Between Japan and South Africa,*(Praeger,2002)
31 http://zaf.mofa.go.kr/english/af/zaf/bilateral/bilateral/index.jsp The Embassy of the Republic of Korea to the Republic of South Africa

orary Aryans seemed to be based more so on Hitler's theories on racial superiority as opposed to mere financial expediency.

This recognition was canonized in Anti-Comintern Pact on Communism which was signed in 1936. Hitler said: "Pride in one's own race – and that does not imply contempt for other races – is also a normal and healthy sentiment. I have never regarded the Chinese or the Japanese as being inferior to ourselves. They belong to ancient civilizations, and I admit freely that their past history is superior to our own. They have the right to be proud of their past, just as we have the right to be proud of the civilization to which we belong. Indeed, I believe the more steadfast the Chinese and the Japanese remain in their pride of race, the easier I shall find it to get on with them."[32]

These sentiments likely result from imbibing the master race theory of Arthur De Gobineau in his, Inequality of the Human Races. It was he in the 19th century who recalibrated the boundaries of whiteness diving whites into three categories: 1) Nordic; 2) Alpine; and 3) Mediterranean. He also declared that civilization in any given people is commensurate with the amount of Aryan blood they have. The Chinese, due to their color, are assumed to possess a lot. Hitler's fellow ideologue and propagandist Heinrich Himmler saw parallels between the Japanese mythology that the Daimyo and Samurai castes were of celestial origin. To Himmler there seemed to be a similarity with the Nazis own myths that the Aryan race were also of celestial origin and descended to earth in order to settle and develop the lost continent of Atlantis.[33] This seemed to explain the Japanese obvious superiority over other Asian and Non-Asian peoples.

Even certain Jews were classified as honorary Aryans by the same Nazi regime that was responsible for their wholesale slaughter in the *Shoah*. One of the founders of the SS, Emile Maurice was later discovered to have Jewish ancestry. He was conveniently given the status of honorary Aryan by Adolf Hitler himself and pardoned for this case of Murphy's Law in genetics.

---

32   The Political Testament of Adolf Hitler, Note #5, (February–April 1945)
33   The Activities of Dr. Ernst Schaefer, OI – Final Interrogation Report (OI-FIR) No. 32, Secret – United States Forces European Theater Military Intelligence Service Center APO 757, February 12, 1946, p. 4.

This was not the only instance of the Third Reich overlooking Jewish ancestry though. Erhad Milch, who was a ranking officer of the Luftwaffe, was half-Jewish as his father Anton Milch was Jewish. His mother later claimed that his father was in fact her uncle who sexually abused her. Cambridge University researcher Bryan Rigg discovered some 1200 Jewish soldiers who served in the Third Reich with Hitler's approval. Among them were 2 full generals, 8 lieutenant generals, and 5 major generals. This arbitrary granting of Aryan race status was so widespread that Gestapo chief Göring famously said: "Wer Jude ist, bestimme ich"(I decide who is a Jew).

This idea of *Japanese Exceptionalism* was also expressed by President Theodore Roosevelt who once said: "Japan is the only nation in Asia that understands the principles and methods of Western civilization." Roosevelt manifested his thoughts into action when he approved the Japan-Korea Treaty of 1905. This practically ended Korean sovereignty and made Korea a protectorate of the Empire of Japan. The United States Supreme Court however weren't as gracious to Japanese-Americans and denied naturalization to Takao Ozawa on the basis that he wasn't Caucasian by the dictates of the law in the decision of Ozawa Vs the United States. Ozawa had argued that Japanese were in fact "Free Whites." The story of the egregious internment of Japanese-Americans during World War II is another such example of the apparent American love/hate relationship with people of Japanese ancestry.

Even Irish and Jews in America just "became" white in America rather recently. There are serious discussions in various Jewish seminaries in America as to whether the amalgamation into "whiteness" in America post-Civil Rights Movement was worth the tradeoff. What these examples of nation-states moving people in and outside of race proves is that the taxonomy of race is not an immutable, physical reality. It is totally subjective and as stated earlier a social construct. A construct that no doubt has real life and social implications for those not in the halls of power. Unfortunately Muslims being a people who have been largely colonized, have like colonized people often do, taken on these ethos which are foreign to their tradition, and have embodied them more than the people who imparted these ideals on them. The umbrage which we expect as a result of such work is grounded in this embodiment of these ideals.

According to the scientific definition of race, race is a species level taxonomy. That is to say that there is but one race for the Homo Sapien Sapiens genus, and that is the human race. What the laity now recognizes as different races are not scientific races determined by phenome. They are mere ethnic identities that are not static and interchangeable as we have demonstrated. The nation-state (which is a European construct) changes who fits into race at its own will. Race is also negotiated by the people themselves. For example many eastern immigrants have elected to change their "race" on the 2020 census forms. The new racial category of MENA (Middle Eastern, North African) will be an option for those who choose to cast aside the racial designation of white.

The history of how Arabs became white in the U.S. is interesting to say the least. Legal scholar Khaled Beydoun who is an Associate Professor of Law at Berry University, has researched the history of Arab racialization in the United States and is an expert in the field of race and law. He has written extensively on how religion played an integral role in Arabs being classified as whites. When commenting on the 53 naturalization hearings involving Arabs from the racially restrictive Naturalization Era (1790-1952), Beydoun says: "Judges during the Naturalization Era viewed "Arab" as synonymous with "Muslim" identity. Because Muslims were presumed to be non-white, and Arabs were presumed to be Muslims, Arabs were presumptively ineligible for citizenship. But this presumption could be rebutted. Arab Christians could – and did – invoke the fact of their Christianity to argue that they were white. These arguments sometimes secured citizenship for Christian petitioners, but did not always rebut the presumption that every immigrant from the Arab World was Muslim. Legal scholars have paid insufficient attention to the Arab naturalization cases. These cases reveal not only how judges viewed religion as a proxy for race, but also the ways in which they conflated Arab identity with Muslim identity to do so."[34]

What we have demonstratively shown with the previous examples is that there are many factors and variables which consti-

34   http://papers.ssrn.com/sol3/papers.cfm?abstract_id=2529506

tute "race" as used by the laity and governments alike, and color phenome is not remotely the defining marker in race. We say all of this to say that there is no such thing as an Arab "race" (that is defined strictly along phenome) or any other race besides the human race.

History of Arab-Black Literature

This project is not the first project of its kind. Since antiquity there has been an entire genre of Arabic literature dealing with "blackness" that is negotiating and expounding upon the relationship of Arab people and dark skin color. The era of Arab history known as "jahilia" or the Age of Ignorance (pre-Islam) is known for a number of Black poets known as "Aghribat-Al-Arab" or the Crows of the Arabs. These were men who were known to have been extremely black. Amongst them were: Antarah from the tribe of Abs, Khafaf bin Nabda from Banu Sulaym, Abu Umair ibn Al-Hubaab and Umair ibn Abu Umair, and Abdullah ibn Khazim, all from Banu Sulaym. Sulaik ibn Sulaka from Banu Tamim, Hishan ibn Uqba ibn Abi Mu'eet, Hammam ibn Muatrraf from Banu Taghlib, Muntashir ibn Wahb Al-Baahili, Matar ibn Awfaa, Al-Mazini, Taabbata Sharra, Al-Shanfara.

It is commonly held that these poets were the sons of Black African slave women and that accounted for their dark hue. This sentiment was expressed in many books of old also. These poets were said to have written about the pain and consternation they felt as a result of their blackness. Not all of these men were mixed ethnically. Although some texts for example list Khafaf bin Nadba as having an Ethiopian mother. However we find that Ibn Sa'ad in his famous Tabaqat" says:

ابن الحارث بن شريد واسمه عمرو بن رباح بن يقظة بن
عصية بن خفاف بن امرئ القيس بن بهثة بن سليم وكان

شاعرا وهو الذي يقال له خفاف بن ندبة وهي أمة بها يعرف وهى ابنة الشيطان بن قنان سبية من بني الحارث بن كعب ويقال إن ندية كانت سوداء وشهد خفاف فتح مكة مع رسول الله صلى الله عليه وسلم وكان معه لواء بني سليم الأخر.

Khafaf the son of Umair the son of Al-Harith the son of Amru (Shuraid) the son of Rabbah the son of Yaqidha the son of Asiyya the son of Khafaf the son of Imr Al-Qais the son of Bahtha the son of Sulaym. He was a poet and was called Khafaf the son of Nadba and Nadba is a slave-girl and Khafaf was known by her. She (Nadba) is the daughter of Al-Shaytan the son of Qanan and she was captured from the tribe of Bani Al-Harith ibn Ka'ab. It is said that Nadba was black-skinned. Khafaf was present with the Prophet ﷺ during the conquest of Mecca and he carried the flag of the tribe of Sulaym.

The great Shafi scholar of hadith Ibn Hajar Asqalani says about his lineage in "Tamyeez al-Sahaba: "

خفاف بن عمير بن الحارث بن الشريد بن رياح بن يقظة بن عصية بن خفاف بن امرئ القيس بن بهثة بن سليم وهو المعروف بابن ندبة بنون وهي أمه قال بن الكلبي شهد الفتح وكان معه لواء بني سليم وكان شاعرًا مشهورا وقال الأصمعي شهد حنينًا وثبت على إسلامه في الردة وبقي إلى زمن عمر وقال أبو عبيدة أغار الحارث بن الشريد يعني جد خفاف هذا على بني الحارث بن كعب فسبي ندبة فوهبها لابنه عمير فولدت له خفافا فنسب إليها قال المرزباني هي ندبة بنت أبان بن شيطان بن قنان بن سلمة.

22

Khafaf the son of Umair the son of Al-Harith the son of Shuraid the son of Rabbah the son of Yaqidha the son of Asiyya the son of Khafaf the son of Imr Al-Qais the son of Bahtha the son of Sulaym. He was a famous poet. Al-Asma'ee said that he was present at the battle of Hunain and that he remained a Muslim during period of apostasy and he was still alive during the reign of Umar. Abu Ubayda said that Al-Harith the son of Shuraid — the grandfather of Khafaf — raided the tribe of Bani Al-Harith ibn Ka'ab and captured Nadba and gave her to his son Umair and she gave birth to Khafaf through Umair and Khafaf was called the son of Nadba. Al-Mirzbaani says that she is Nadba the daughter of Abaan the son of Al-Shaytan the son of Qanan the son of Salama. Bani Al-Harith ibn Ka'ab is a large Arab tribe and Al-Harith ibn Ka'ab is the son of Amru the son of 'Illa the son of Khalid the son of Midhhaj.

The Hajin and Scriptural Analysis of Black Loathing in Jahili Poetry

Even if we ignore the historical descriptions of Khafaf and other of the black jahili poets being of pure Arab ancestry and not mixed Arab/African ancestry, this would not disqualify them from being considered pure Arabs. The Arabs classify themselves into three categories: Arab al-Bad or the Ancient Arabs such as Ad and Thamud, Arab-ul-Aarab or the Pure Yemeni Qahtani stock, and the Musta'arab or the Arabized Arabs. This last category accounts for most of who we now consider Arabs. That is most of the people of the Levant, the Berbers of North Africa, and the Egyptians etc. Pre-Islamic Arab society was not one without a hierarchy. Arab society was a caste-based, patriarchal society where lineage was prized and traced via the man.

If a child was sired by an Arab man via a non-Arab woman and the man acknowledged paternity than the child was considered an Arab and a member of the tribe. The sons of slave women no matter the complexion or ethnicity of the mother would fall under the category of hajin. Bernard Lewis expounds on the hajin when speaking of the caste when he says: "Hajin would indicate a horse whose sire was a thoroughbred and whose dam was not. It had much the same meaning when applied to human beings, denoting a person whose father was Arab and free and whose mother was a slave. The term haijn in social rather than racial in content, expressing contempt of the highborn for the baseborn, without attributing any specific racial identity to the latter. Non-Arabs, of whatever racial origin, were of course baseborn but so too were many Arabs who, for one reason or another, were not full free and members of a tribe. Full Arabs-those born of two free Arab parents-ranked above half-Arabs, the children of Arab fathers and non-Arab mothers (the opposite was inadmissible). In turn, half-Arabs ranked above non-Arabs, who were, so to speak out of the system." [35]

So we see that being Arab had nothing to do with their complexion, rather it was determined by whether their fathers were Arab and or whether their mother was free. Lewis states further that: "At his discretion, the free father of a slave could recognize and liberate him and thus confer membership in the tribe."[36] In the case of Khufaf, he became a noble and leader of his tribe, so his blackness or possible half-African ancestry was not an impediment which negated his Arabness or social mobility. In poems attributed to Antarah and other black poets of the pre-Islamic era, there seems to be some consternation and frustration attributed to their blackness.

For example, in a poem attributed to Antarah we see the following: "I am a man, of whom one half ranks with the best of the Abs. The other half, I defend with my sword."[37]

In another set of verses attributed to him he says: "I am the son of a black-browed woman

Like the hyena that thrives on an abandoned camping ground, her leg is like the leg of an ostrich, and her hair like peppercorns, her front teeth gleam behind her veil like lightening, in curtained darkness."

The second poem is problematic to say the least as it implies that Antarah is describing his mother in a disrespectful and pejorative manner. Dr. Bernard Lewis contends that these poems were later additions. His stance is that these verses are indicative of a social reality that was not present during the pre-Islamic era. That is to say that pre-Islamic Arab society didn't have an ingrained anti-black sentiment.

---

35   http://www.artsrn.ualberta.ca/amcdouga/MEAS200/readings_topic2_2006/crows_of_the_arabs_lewis.pdf

36   ibid

37   Wilhelm Ahlwardt, ed, *The Diwans of the Six Ancient Arabic Poets Ennabigha, 'Antarah Tharafa, Zuhair, 'Alqama, and ImrulQais* (London 1870), p 42. See *Encyclopedia of Islam*, 2d., s.v. "Antarah."

Arabia, Africans &
Historical Intersections

Arabs themselves were in fact conquered by Ethiopians[38] who had a more sophisticated culture. They had a written language which had the same ancient origins as Arabic. Written Ge'ez was probably more widespread than written Arabic at the time. The

Arabic characters which are currently used today only became standardized a short time before the birth of Muhammad ﷺ. It was related by both Ibn Sa'd and Ibn Abi Shaybah on the authority of as-Sha'abi who said: "The first amongst the Arabs (descendants of Ishmael) to write the Arabic language was Harb ibn Umayyah ibn Abdu Shams, the father of Abu Sufyan. It was said to him, 'From where did you learn this?' He said, 'From the people of Hira.' It was said, 'And from whom did the people of Hira learn it?' He said, 'From the people of Anbar.'" Hira and Anbar were cities of antiquity located along the Euphrates River in Iraq. It was related by Waki'u in his al-Gharar.

The Aksumite (modern day Ethiopia) kingdom held the territory of Yemen and as far east as Najran. The Quran speaks about a group of believers who were incinerated in a case of religious persecution. The Himyarite King Dhu Nuwas rebelled against the Ethiopian rulers of the Arabian Peninsula in and around 522 C.E. and began attacking the garrison cities of Zafar and Mukhawan. Najran suffered one of the worst atrocities in which hundreds of people were burned alive because of their refusal to abandon

---

38   Glen W. Bowersock, *The Rise and Fall of a Jewish Kingdom in Arabia*, Institute Journal of Institute of Advanced Study Fall 2011 Issue

their faith. This incident is recorded in the 85th chapter of the Quran called: "Surah Al-Buruj." According to many historians these people were mainly Ethiopian Christians.[39] Muslim scholars such as Imams Ibn Jawzi (d.1201 C.E.) and Imam Jalul-ul-Din Suyuti(d. 1505) both stated that the *Companions of the Ditch* as they are referred to in the Quran were in fact Ethiopian.

So esteemed were the Ethiopians in the eyes of Arab/Islamic historians and exegesis that Suyuti said that every probative verse in the Quran about Christians was specifically revealed about the Ethiopians, those of the pre-Islamic period as the case of the *Companions of the Ditch* as well as Muhammad's ☙ contemporary King Ashama ibn Abjar as he is known according to Arabic sources. This name corresponds to the Ge'ez name Ella Seham which is a variant of Sahama. Basic knowledge of plate tectonics informs us that Western Arabia was once part of the African land mass. Between Yemen and Somalia there is but 14 miles of water now separating them. Encyclopedia Britannica itself states that: "The southern region of the peninsula (Arabia) has more a greater affinity with Somalia and Ethiopia in Africa than with Northern Arabia or the rest of Asia."[40]

It seems to be nothing less than a historical and cultural hit job that the Arabian Peninsula is not generally classified as Africa although it's clearly connected to Africa but Madagascar is considered Africa despite the fact that it isn't. Noted historian and scholar Ali Mazruri states very plainly: "a European decision to make Africa end at the Red Sea has decisively de-Africanized the Arabian Peninsula...the tyranny of the sea is in part a tyranny of European geographical prejudices. Just as European map-makers could decree that on the map Europe was above Africa instead of below (an arbitrary decision in relation to the cosmos) those map-makers could also dictate that Africa ended at the Red Sea instead of the Persian Gulf. Is it not time that this dual tyranny

---

39 Christopher Haas, 'Geopolitics and Georgian Identity in Late Antiquity: The Dangerous World of Vakhtang Gorgasali,' in Tamar Nutsubidze, Cornelia B. Horn, Basil Lourié(eds.),Georgian Christian Thought and Its Cultural Context, BRILL pp.29-44, p.36-39
40 Encyclopedia Britanica s.v. Arabian Desert. Britanica Online at http://www.britannica.com/EBchecked/topic/31610/Arabian-Desert. Accessed February 12, 2009.

of the sea and Eurocentric geography was forced to sink to the bottom?"[41]

At any rate black phenotype was not something strange to the Arabs. This stance is not a case of Afrocentric eisegesis. The Arab polymath Al-Jahiz(d. 868 C.E.) in his work " Fakhr-ul-Sawdan-Ala-Badan" (The Glory of the Blacks over the Whites) was of the first Islamic writers who said similar statements centuries before. Al-Jahiz noted that the Bani Sulaym themselves were black in complexion when he said: "God may He be exalted did not make them black in order to disfigure them; rather it is their environment which made them so. The best evidence of this is that there are black tribes amongst the Arabs, such as the Bani Sulaym bin Mansur, and all of the people who settled in the Harra, besides the Bani Sulaym are black. These tribes take slaves from amongst the Ashban to mend their flocks and for irrigation work, manual labor, and domestic service, and they take their wives from among the Byzantines; and yet it takes less than three generations for the Harra region to give them all the complexion of the Bani Sulaym."

---

41   Ali A. Mazrui, Euro-Jews and Afro-Arabs: The Great Semitic Divergence in World History (Lanham: University Press of America, 2008) 140

The Linguistic Association between Arabness and Blackness

Arabness and blackness were not viewed as mutually exclusive in early Islamic history. By blackness in this context is not an identity which has been framed as inferior compared to whiteness in the colonial and post-colonial periods but relating to physical traits such as brown or black which can also include curly or kinky hair texture. In fact, the predominant description of Arabs was within the framework of non-white complexion. This point is illustrated in a number of classical Islamic texts both explicitly and implicitly.

In one of the most authoritative lexicons of the Arabic language titled Lisan al-Arab by ibn Manzur, Arabness and blackness are connected. He notes that the skin color of Arabs was primarily known to be as-Sumrah (brown) and al-Udmah whereas the Romans and Persians were known to be al-Bayad (white) and al-Humrah.[42] Al-Udmah, which is related to the word Adam, carries the meaning of dark brown relating to skin tone for people.[43] Additionally, Al-Humrah, which is related to Ahmar and literally means red, has the association of light skin tone or whiteness.

Al-Jahiz, a black Iraqi scholar who lived in the same era as famous jurists ash-Shafi'i and Ahmad bin Hanbal, also commented on another Prophetic narration of "I was sent to the white and to the black" by stating, "If they [Arabs] are among the blacks,

---

42   Ibn Manzur, Lisan al-Arab, Volume 4, Page 209
43   Ibn ash-Shajari al-Hasani, Ma Ittifaqa Lafzuhu wa Ikhtilaf Ma'nah, Volume 1, Page 5

then this name was derived from our own name. And they were merely called black in spite of being dark and brown."[44] Al-Jahiz also further elaborated on this point that Bani Sulaym was a tribe from the Hijaz with black skin that was Arab not African. .

An-Nawawi commented on a similar Prophetic tradition referenced by Al-Jahiz stating that one meaning for white (Ahmar) is non-Arab and black means Arab though he did also mention that white means a human while black means jinn. [45]

In yet another narration, a prophecy has manifested itself which compares Arabness with blackness. In a tradition relayed by Al-Hakim and considered authentic by al-Haythami plus is also narrated through 6 different men other hadith collections with slight variances in wording, the Messenger of Allah stated:

I saw myself in a dream following a herd of black sheep then white sheep came among them.

> Abu Bakr said, "Oh Messenger of Allah! It is the Arabs who you are following then later the non-Arabs until they will overwhelm the Arabs in number." The Prophet replied to him that an angel interpreted the dream the same way.[46]

Yet another example relating to association of Arabness and blackness in contrast to non-Arabness and whiteness is seen in the famous poem "Jiymiyyah" written by the prolific poet of the Abbasi era named ibn ar-Rumi. The poem contains a response to the Abbasi khalifah al-Mutawakkil who desecrated the grave of Imam al-Husayn bin Ali and prevented people from visiting it upon the threat of death. In this same time period, Yahya bin Umar bin al-Husayn bin Zayd bin Ali bin al-Husayn bin Ali bin Abi Talib, who was described as being dark brown in skin color, revolted against the Abbasi government. He composed to Al-Mutawakkil:

> You insult [the descendants of Prophet Muhammad] due to their blackness while they are pure Arabs with black completion. However, you are

---

44   Al-Jahiz, *Risa'il Al-Jahiz*, Volume 1, Page 156

45   An-Nawawi, *Sharh Sahih Muslim*, No. 520

46   Al-Hakim an-Nisaburi, *Al-Mustadarik As-Sahihayn*, No. 8264

blue [eyed] – the Roman people have embellished
your faces with their color.[47]

Relating to color, al-Abyad which literally means white was
also used by Arabs in times past to describe people in a non-lit-
eral sense, meaning having no relation to skin color. Hence,
Arab poets would praise a person or a people as being noble or
honorable by saying "So and so has a white face."[48] Moreover,
white in this context had no relationship to phenotype but strictly
spiritual character.

---

47   Al-Isfahan, *Maqatil at-Talibin*, Page 428
48   Ibn Manzur, *Lisan al-Arab*, Volume 7, Page 124

The Quran and Ethiopian Vernacular

The great polymath and exemplar of Islamic knowledge, Imam Jalal-ul-Din Suyuti (d. 911 AH), wrote a magnificent work on the words in the Quran which has Ethiopian counterparts and origins. As a matter of fact there is a genre of Arab literature dedicated to showing the cultural continuity and influence of blackness vis-à-vis Arabness dating back to antiquity. Dating back to the previous mentioned "Ghurab Al-Arab" (Black Crows of the Arabs) there has been many works dealing with these subjects. This shouldn't come as a surprise as there is a mere 14 mile separation between the Arabian Peninsula and the Horn of Africa. Ethiopians had colonized Arabia in antiquity and the blood lines of the Arab-ul-Bad (Ancient Arabs) and the Arab-ul-A'Arab have long been mixed. The name of one of these such valuable works is entitled "The Elevation of the Affair of the Ethiopians", and below are a few excerpts dealing with the linguistic connection between the eternal speech of Allah and African people.

Muhammad bin Abu Tahir Al-Bazzaz, told us on the authority of Abu Musa that he said: " The word 'kiflayn' in Surah Hadid verse 28 is an Ethiopian word meaning *di fayn* (re-doubling) in Arabic."

Ibn Qutayba and Muhammad ibn Abdul Baqi bin Ahmad, told us on the authority of Sa'id ibn Iyad said that the word (*mishkah*) means *al-kuwah* (skylight in Arabic).

Umar said that Umar bin Abu Zayada said that: " I heard that Ikrima say that 'Ta ha' means O Mankind (man) in Ethiopian.

Waki said that on the authority of Ibn Abbas that: "*Inna nashi'at al-layl*" from Surah Muzzamil verse 6 means "if he wishes he stands," in the Ethiopian language. The companion Ibn Masud, said that it means "*qiyam-ul-layl* or getting ready to stand for the night. Al-Zajaj said that it means: "Any part of the night hours, or any part you want from it."

Abdul Wahab ibn Mubarak said that "*awwah*" in the verse: "Surely Abraham was forbearing, grieving and constantly returning too Allah" (11:75) means "*mumin* or believer in Ethiopia."

Among the sayings of the Prophet ﷺ in his speech which were Ethiopian are the following,

Narrated Abu Hurayra, The Prophet ﷺ said: "Religious knowledge will be taken away by the death of the scholars and *harj* will increase." He ﷺ was asked what is "*harj*?" and he ﷺ responded: 'killing'. *Harj* is an Ethiopian word meaning killing (Sahih Bukhari, Book of Signs of the Day of Judgment.).

In another narration found in the Book of Dress in the Sahih of Bukhari:

حَدَّثَنَا حِبَّانُ بْنُ مُوسَى، أَخْبَرَنَا عَبْدُ اللهِ، عَنْ خَالِدِ بْنِ سَعِيدٍ، عَنْ أَبِيهِ، عَنْ أُمِّ خَالِدٍ بِنْتِ خَالِدِ بْنِ سَعِيدٍ، قَالَتْ أَتَيْتُ رَسُولَ اللهِ صلى الله عليه وسلم مَعَ أَبِي وَعَلَيَّ قَمِيصٌ أَصْفَرُ، قَالَ رَسُولُ اللهِ صلى الله عليه وسلم «سَنَهْ سَنَهْ». قَالَ عَبْدُ اللهِ وَهْىَ بِالْحَبَشِيَّةِ حَسَنَةٌ

Narrated Um Khalid: (the daughter of Khalid bin Sa`id) I went to Allah's Apostle with my father and I was wearing a yellow shirt. Allah's Apostle said, "Sanah, Sanah!" (`Abdullah, the narrator, said that 'Sanah' meant 'good' in the Ethiopian language).

From these examples we see the familiarity and closeness of the Ethiopian language to the speech of Allah and the Messenger of Allah ﷺ himself.

Imam Ali bin Abi Talib
Brother of the Prophet

A man of faith, courage, austerity and knowledge in the way of the Prophet was Imam Ali bin Abi Talib.

Imam Ali was born in Makkah in the Ka'bah during the Era of Ignorance. His father was Abu Talib, the paternal uncle and protector of the Prophet in Makkah, and his mother was Fatimah bint Asad, the woman who also raised the Prophet like a son.

The majority description of Imam Ali in Sunni, Isma'ili and Ja'fari texts is that he was extremely dark (*adam shahid al-udmah*) or black in skin color.[49] Other texts including from the Zaydi school of thought describe him as being closest in skin color to brown.[50]

Ahmad bin Hanbal stated that there were no more virtues narrated with sound chains of narrations about any from among the companions than for Imam Ali.[51] He is an imam of Sunni

49 Al-Khatib Al-Baghdadi, Tarikh al-Baghdadi, Juz 1, Page 145
   Al-Mizzi, Tahdhib al-Kamal, Juz 20, Page 480
   Ibn al-Athir, Al-Kamal fi at-Tarikh, Juz 3, Page 396
   Adh-Dhahabi, Tarikh al-Islam, Juz 3, Page 624
   Ibn al-Jawzi, Sifah as-Safwah, Page 116
   Ibn Sa'ad, At-Tabaqat al-Kubra, Juz 3, Page 27
   Al-Qadi an-Nu'man, Sharh Al-Akhbar, Juz 2, Page 427
   Ibn Shar Ashub, Manaqib Aali Abi Talib, Juz 3, Page 91
   Al-Khawarizmi, Al-Manaqib, Page 45
   Al-Majlisi, Bihar al-Anwar, Juz 35, Page 2
50 Ibn Mansur al-Mu'ayyidi, *At-Tuhf Sharh az-Zalaf*, Page 24
51 Ibn al-Jawzi, *Manaqib al-Imam Ahmad bin Hanbal*, Page 163

and Shi'i muslims alike, and his opinions and sayings are even quoted in madhhab Ibadi, a school of thought practiced in Oman, Tanzania and parts of North Africa that is mistakenly referred to as modern day Khawarij. Moreover, virtually every spiritual (Sufi) order (At-Tijaniyyah, Al-Ba Alawiyyah, An-Naqshabandi al-Aliyyah, etc) traces its knowledge through the chain of Imam Ali.

There is no other Islamic personality who has been written about more than Imam Ali except for Prophet Muhammad. Given his biography is so vast, here are aspects of the life of Imam Ali that are widely narrated:

He was raised in the household of the Prophet, which includes before and after the revealing of the Qur'an.

He was the first male to accept Islam and the first to pray with the Prophet.

He lied in the bed of the Prophet ﷺ the night that the Prophet left Makkah to Al-Madinah. Quraysh then beat him up because he spoiled their plot to murder the Prophet.

When the Prophet paired off companions in Al-Madinah to be best friends, he left Imam Ali for himself and said, "You are my brother in the dunya and the next-life."

When the Prophet ﷺ left Imam Ali in charge of the affairs of Al-Madinah before heading off to Ghazwah Tabuk, he told him, "You are to me in the position of Harun to Musa though there is no prophet after me."

Upon the passing of the Prophet, Imam Ali performed the ghusl as well as the funeral prayer.

During the governments of Abu Bakr and Umar, Imam Ali gave them the wisest of council. Umar famously said, "'Umar would have been ruined if it were not for Ali."

During the revolt against Uthman while he was the khalifah, Imam Ali sent his sons to his home to protect him. During a siege, 'Uthman was later killed.

Imam Ali was the fourth khalifah and given allegiance by the majority of the Ummah including the People of the Hijaz, Yemen and Iraq.

He is credited with being the first to systematize the grammar of the Arabic language and was the teacher of the top scholars of the second generation of Muslims including Abu Al-Aswad Ad-Duwali, Al-Hasan Al-Basri and Mujahid bin Jabr.

He was martyred during Ramadan at the time of fajr prayer in Al-Kufah, Iraq by the Khariji named Abdur Rahman bin Muljam.

Here are a few of the many statements of wisdom and legal rulings of Imam Ali:

"Knowledge is better than wealth. Knowledge guards you while you guard your wealth."[52]

When asked if the People of al-Jamal & Siffin (patrons of Mu'awiyah bin Abi Sufyan) and an-Nahrawan (the Khawarij) were disbelievers, he replied that they are our brothers who rebelled against us and that we will fight them until they return to the command of Allah Might and Sublime.[53]

It is not in the Qur'an the saying "Oh you who believe" except that in the Torah mentioned "Oh you impoverish."[54]

"Your friends are three and your adversaries are three. Your friends are your direct friend, the friend of your friend, and the adversary of your adversary. Your adversaries are your direct adversary, the adversary of your friend, and the friend of your adversary."[55]

"Surely the rich is the rich in his heart... The rich is not the rich in his wealth"

"And thus the generous is the honorable in his character... The generous is not just with his people and family"

"And thus the comprehending is knowledgeable of his condition... The comprehending is not just with his discourse and speech."[56]

"The one who is pleased with the action of a people is like the one who enters into it with them."[57]

---

52   Ibn al-Jawzi, *Sifwah as-Safwah*, Page 122

53   Zayd bin Ali, *Musnad al-Imam Zayd*, Pages 395–396

54   Ali bin Musa, *Sahifah al-Imam ar-Rida*, Page 70

55   Az-Zamakhshari, *Rabi'a al-Abrar wa Fusus al-Akhbar fi al-Muhadarat*, Juz 1, Page 191

56   Ali bin Abi Talib, *Diwan al-Imam Ali bin Abi Talib*, Page 114

57   Ash-Sharif ar-Radi, *Khasa'is Amir al-Mu'minin Ali bin Abi Talib*, Page 88

"When you see the black flags, remain where you are and do not move your hands nor feet. Thereafter there shall appear a feeble people to whom no concern is given. Their hearts will be like fragments of iron. They are the representatives of the state (ad-Dawlah). They will not fulfill their covenant and their agreement. They will call to the truth though they are not from its people. Their names will be a kunya [i.e., Abu Such and Such], and their ascriptions will be to towns [i.e. Al-Baghdadi]. Their hair will be long like that of women. [They shall be so] until they dispute among themselves, then Allah will bring forth the truth from whomever He wills."[58]

---

58   Nu'aym bin Hammad, *Kitab al-Fitan*, Hadith Number 573

Ammar bin Yasir

The Man who the Prophet Predicted his Martyrdom

One of the companions who has several narrated merits pertaining to his faith, personality and resilience is Ammar bin Yasir.

Ammar is described in Al-Mustadarak ala As-Sahihayn by Al-Hakim and authenticated by Adh-Dhahabi as being tall in stature, black in skin color and having kinky hair.[59] His father Yasir was Arab.

Ammar was one of the earliest Muslims to accept Islam and was regularly tortured along with his family. Once while being severely tortured, he unwillingly recanted Islam. He later came to the Prophet in a state of tears saying that he verbally recanted Islam but did not mean it, in which the Prophet wiped away his tears and recited surah 16, ayah 106, "Whoever disbelieves in Allah after belief except who is forced and whose heart is still content with faith..." This account is narrated in virtually every book of tafsir of the Qur'an.

After much persecution, Ammar with other companions migrated to Abyssinia finding protection under a just Christian king though ibn Ishaq disputes that he was one of those companions in Abyssinia. He later migrated with other companions to Al-Madinah making him within a select group of companions that made two migrations for the sake of Allah.

Ammar later participated in the major campaigns to protect the Muslim community including Badr and Uhud. He also was

59   Al-Hakim, *Al-Mustadrak ala as-Sahihayn*, Hadith number 5650

a witness to the Farewell Pilgrimage and the event of Ghadir Khumm.

Prior to the death of the Prophet, he told Ammar, "You will be killed by a group of transgressors." This hadith is sahih and mutawatir, meaning narrated so widely by many sound people that it is beyond doubt.

During the government of Umar bin Al-Khattab, Ammar was nominated to be the governor of Kufah in Iraq to be later removed from his position when Umar consolidated the governorship of Kufah with Basrah under Abu Musa Al-Ashari.

During the government of Ali bin Abi Talib, Ammar accompanied Imam Ali's army at the Battle of Jamal and defended him against the Khawarij movement, the original takfiris. Ammar later achieved martyrdom at the Battle of Siffin by being killed by a man from the army of Mu'awiyah bin Abi Sufyan.[60]

---

60   Ibn al-Jawzi, *Sifah as-Safwah*, Page 161

Sumayyah

The First Martyr from the Companions

The early history of Islam in Makkah is marked by many stellar and courageous women. One of the foremost of them during this era was Sumayyah bint Khayyat.

Sumayyah was enslaved by Abu Hudhayfah bin Al-Mughirah to be later emancipated after her marriage to Yasir who was an Arab.[61] Through her union with Yasir, she birthed a son named Ammar. Like Sumayyah who was described as black, her son Ammar was described as having black skin with kinky hair.

Sumayyah was one of the earliest persons to accept Islam in Makkah, and she was one of the oppressed who was routinely tortured along with other non-Qurayshi Muslims such as Bilal and Khabbab. When the Prophet would pass by them being tortured by Quraysh in the intense heat, he would say to them, "Patience Oh Family of Yasir, for your destination of paradise."[62]

One of these days of torture when Sumayyah and her family were being brutally mistreated for not recanting Islam and refusing to submit to worshiping idols, Abu Jahl, the uncle and archenemy of the Prophet, stabbed Sumayyah.

On that fateful day, Sumayyah became the first companion of the Prophet to achieve martyrdom.

---

61   Ibn Hibban, *Tarikh as-Sahabah*, Page 130
62   Ibn al-Jawzi, *Sifwah as-Saffah*, Page 160

43

Umm Ayman

Mother after the Prophet's Mother

The companion of the Prophet named Barakah, meaning blessing, otherwise known as Umm Ayman was Abyssinian and a servant of Abdullah bin Abdil Muttalib, the father of the Prophet.[63] When Aminah, the mother of the Prophet died, Umm Ayman took over as primary care-giver of the Prophet. Hence, the Prophet referred to her "Umm Ayman is my mother after my [biological] mother."[64]

Umm Ayman was later emancipated at the time of the marriage of the Prophet to Sayyidah Khadijah bint Khuwaylid.[65]

Umm Ayman was one of the early adherents of Islam in Makkah and was one of those who faced persecution from Quraysh. She was among those who migrated from Makkah to Abyssinia then to Al-Madinah.

Umm Ayman's first marriage was to Ubayd who was from Bani Khazraj, a prominent tribe in the Hijaz. Umm Ayman and Ubayd, who was black, had a son named Ayman who was also black.[66] Ubayd was martyred at Ghazwah Khaybar, and Ayman was martyred at Ghazwah Hunayn. Umm Ayman participated in Ghazwah Uhud and Ghazwah Khaybar.

After Ubayd's martyrdom, it is reported that the Prophet said to the companions that if anyone wanted to marry a lady

---

63   Ibn Hibban, *Tarikh as-Sahabah*, Page 49
64   Muslim, *Sahih Muslim*, Number 2453
65   Ibn al-Jawzi, *Sifah as-Safwah*, Page 303
66   Ibn Hajar, *Kitab al-Isabah*, Juz 1, Page 170

from the People of Paradise then marry Umm Ayman. Zayd bin Harithah the man who the Prophet emancipated and raised like a son, was then married to Umm Ayman.[67] Though Zayd was Arab and there are some conflicting descriptions about his physical appearance, authentic sources state that Zayd was short with a flat nose and had dark skin.[68]

Umm Ayman had a particularly close relationship to Ahl al-Bayt, the Household of the Prophet. She shared intimate moments with Ahl al-Bayt such as being present at the marriage that the Prophet conducted between his daughter Sayyidah Fatimah and Imam Ali. At the time of the passing of the Prophet, she grieved alongside Ahl al-Bayt.

There are conflicting narrations about Umm Ayman's passing.

---

67   Ibn Sa'ad, *At-Tabaqat al-Kubra*, Number 10345
68   Ibn al-Jawzi, *Tanwir al-Ghabash*, Page 131

Hamamah

One of the Early Female Companions

One of the early companions who sacrificed for the sake of Allah was Hamamah Al-Habashiyyah.

Hamamah was born in Abyssinia as a free person but was later enslaved by a man from Quraysh after the forces of the Abyssinia emperor Abraha were defeated in Arabia. While enslaved, she was able to marry Rabah, who was an Arab.

It is narrated that Abu Umar stated in Al-Isbah by ibn Hajar Al-Asqalani that Hamamah was torture because of her belief in Allah ﷻ, thus is a testimony that she was recognized as being Muslim. She was freed from slavery by Abu Bakr.[69]

Abu Ali Al-Ghassani stated that this woman of honor was the mother of Bilal the Prayer Caller, who the Prophet gave the title Master of the Prayer Callers.

---

69   Ibn Hajr, *Al-Isbah*, Volume 8, Page 88

Abu Dharr
Man of Moral Courage

One of the honorable companions, who is known for his faithfulness and concern for the poor was Abu Dharr.

Abu Dharr's full name was Jundab bin Junadah from the Tribe of Ghifar.[70] He was described by ibn Sa'ad in At-Tabaqat Al-Kubra and others as being tall with brown (asmar) skin.[71]

In the Era of Ignorance, the Ghifari tribe was known for banditry and alcohol consumption besides worshiping idols. Abu Dharr, however, turned away from these tribal norms even before embracing Islam.

When a man from his tribe informed his people that he saw a man in Makkah, meaning the Prophet ﷺ, who he saw enjoining good and forbidding evil, Abu Dharr set off for Makkah.[72] After meeting the Prophet ﷺ, Abu Dharr swiftly accepted Islam. He went to the Ka'bah to publicly declare his faith in which Quraysh proceeded to beat him. He went the following day to proclaim his faith again in which he was beaten again. After days of doing this and facing beatings, the Prophet ﷺ told him to go back to his tribe, so he could declare his message to them.

He later migrated to Al-Madinah and participated in Ghazwah Badr and other expeditions with the companions.

During the government of Uthman, Abu Dharr was one of the outspoken companions against the lavish lifestyle and large

70   Ibn Hibban, *Tarikh as-Sahabah*, Page 60
71   Ibn Sa'ad, *At-Tabaqat al-Kubra*, Volume 4, Page 432
72   Al-Bukhari, *Sahih al-Bukhari*, Hadith Number 3522

amounts of money which particular Muslims were receiving from the treasury. After conflict between Abu Dharr and Marwan in Al-Hakam, a cousin of Uthman, over a payment that he received of 500,000 dirhams, Abu Dharr was sent away from Al-Madinah to Damascus. While in Damascus, Abu Dharr continued to speak out against luxuries and neglect of the poor which brought him into conflict with the Governor of Damascus, Mu'awiyah bin Abi Sufyan, who was also a cousin of Uthman.

The Prophet said, "May Allah have mercy upon Abu Darr. He will walk alone, die alone, and be resurrected alone."[73] This prediction of his living and dying manifested itself. Due to the circumstances of the time, Abu Dharr left Damascus for Ar-Rabathah desert with virtual no possessions in which he eventually died alone.

---

73   Ibn Kathir, *Al-Bidayah wa an-Nihayah*, 5/8

Lady Fidda
Servant of Ahl al-Bayt

Lady Fidda was originally from Ethiopia, it has been narrated that she was of royal blood but was captured and brought to Arabia. She was freed by the Holy Prophet ﷺ and afterwards served Sayyidina Fatimah ؏ as her maid-servant. Sayyidina Fatimah ؏ divided her house work equally between herself and Lady Fidda and they would take turns to do the chores. She remained faithful to the household of the Prophet ﷺ and even accompanied them to Kerbala and to prison of Syria. She also had the honor of taking part in the "Three Days Fast". Once, when Imam Hasan and Imam Husain ؏ fell sick, the Prophet ﷺ suggested that Imam Ali ؏ make a vow to fast for three days when the children recovered. When they were better, Imam Ali , Sayyida Fatimah , Imam Hasan, Imam Husain and Lady Fidda all fasted to fulfil the vow.

However, on each of the three days, when they sat to break their fast, a hungry person came to their door pleaded for food. The first said he was poor, the second said he was an orphan and the third said he was a freed captive. Each time, the big-hearted members of the house, including Lady Fidda, gave away their food and broke their fast with water. In praise of this selfless action Allah revealed the 76th Chapter of the Holy Qur'an. The incident is described as follows:

They who fulfil their vows, and fear the day, the woe of which stretches far and wide. And they give away food, out of love for

Him, to the poor and the orphan and the captive, (saying), "We feed you only for the sake of Allah, we do not want anything from you, not even thanks. Verily we fear from our Lord a stern day of distress." So Allah will guard them from the evil of that day and give them freshness and pleasure. (Surah Dahr (Insaan), 76:7–11)

Abdullah Mubarak has related a very interesting dialogue between himself and Lady Fidda.[74] He states, "I saw a woman passing through the desert who had fallen behind the caravan and asked her, "Who are you and where are you from?" She replied:

And say, "*Salaam*" *for they shall soon know!* (Surah Zukhruf, 43:89)

I learned that she expected me to greet her and say "Assalaamu Alaykum" first, before any question. I did as she reminded, and then enquired why she was in the desert. She answered: *And whomsoever Allah guides, there can be none to lead astray!* (Surah Zumar, 39:37)

On hearing her reply, I asked her, "Are you from mankind or from the jinn?" She replied: *O Children of Adam! Be adorned at every time of prostration.* (Surah A'raf, 7:31)

I understood that she was human and then asked her, "Where are you coming from?" She replied: *Those who are called to from a place far off.* (Surah Ha Mim 41:44)

I asked her, "Where are you intending to go?" She said: *And (purely) for Allah, is incumbent upon mankind, the Pilgrimage of the House.* (Surah Al-Imran, 3:97)

I asked her how many days she had been travelling. She told me: *And indeed We (Allah) created the heavens and the earth and what is between them two, in six days.* (Surah Qaaf, 50:38)

I asked her, "Do you feel hungry?" She replied: *We (Allah) did not make them such bodies that ate no food.* (Surah Anbiya, 21:8)

I gave her food and asked her to hurry up to catch the caravan but she replied: *Allah does not task any soul beyond its ability.* (Surah Baqarah, 2:286)

I suggested that she sit on the camel behind me, but she said: *Had there been gods therein besides Allah, there would have been disorder in both (the heavens and the earth).* (Surah Anbiya, 21:22)

---

74 Muhammad Baqir Al-Majlisi *Bihar al-anwar al-jami at li-durar akhbar Al-aimmat Al-athar* (Beirut:Wafa) Vol 45 pg 169

I realized that, because we were not husband and wife, it was Haraam for both of us to ride the camel. So I got off and mounted her on it. As she sat on the camel, she said: *Glory to Him Who subjected this to us.* (Surah Zukhruf 43:13)

When we reached the caravan, I asked her, "Do you know anyone among them?" She called out in reply: *O Dawud, Verily, We have appointed you a vicegerent in the earth.* (Surah Saad, 38:26). *And Muhammad is not but a Messenger."* (Surah Al-Imran, 3:144). *O Yahya! Hold the book with firmness!"* (Surah Maryam, 19:12). *O Musa! Verily I am Allah, the All-Mighty.* (Surah Naml, 27:9)

I began to call out these four names at which four youths came out of the caravan and ran towards Lady Fidda. I asked her who they were and she replied: *Wealth and children are the adornment of the world.* (Surah Kahf, 18:46)

I realized that they were her sons. The woman turned to the youth and said: *O my Father, employ him, verily the best of those who you can employ is the strong man and the trusted one.* (Surah Qasas, 28:26)

She thus made them understand that I had helped her. Then she told them: *And verily God increases manifold to whosoever He wills.* (Surah Baqarah, 2:261)

The sons understood their mother's hint and paid me well. I asked them who this noble lady was, and they replied, "She is our mother, Fidda, the maid-servant of Lady Fatima. She has conversed in nothing but the Holy Qur'an for the last 20 years."[75]

75   Ayatullah Mirza Mahdi Pooya, *Essence of the Holy Quran:The Eternal Light* (Imam Sahab-uz-Zaman Association, 1990)

Al-Miqdad bin Amr
Beloved of the Prophet

Al-Miqdad bin Amr was one of the most beloved companions to the Prophet. He came from the Bahra tribe which originated from Hadramawt, Yemen. Ibn al-Jawzi described him as being "tall and adam (brown)."[76] Al-Jahiz also mentioned him among the most notable black companions of the Prophet.[77]

Al-Miqdad is popularly referred to as al-Miqdad bin al-Aswad; however, this description is not simply due to his skin color. Al-Miqdad left his people at a young age for Makkah and was taken in by al-Aswad al-Kindi.[78] Al-Aswad loved him so much that he began to refer to him as his son. Hence people began to refer to al-Miqdad as al-Miqdad bin Al-Aswad.

Al-Miqdad was one of the early Muslims who accepted Islam in Makkah. When the Prophet faced his life being threatened in Makkah, al-Miqdad stayed steadfast and defended the Prophet at risk to his personal safety. Thus it is narrated in several texts in which one has a good chain of narrators that the Prophet said:

Surely Allah commanded me to love four and informed me that He loves them. It was said, Oh Messenger of Allah, name them for us. He replied, Ali is from them then he said the other three are Abu Dharr, Al-Miqdad and Salman. I was commanded to love them and informed that He loves them.[79]

---

76   Ibn al-Jawzi, Sifah as-Safwah, Page 153
77   Al-Jahiz, Risa'il al-Jahiz, Vol. 1, Page 126
78   Ibn Hibban, Tarikh as-Sahabah, Page 230
79   At-Tirmidhi, Sunan at-Tirmidhi, No. 3718

Al-Miqdad was of those who migrated for the sake of Allah from Makkah to al-Madinah. He was the first companion to ride a horse in a battle, being the only one to mount a horse during the Battle of Badr. He also participated in Uhud and other campaigns.

Al-Miqdad also was married by the Prophet to a noble woman from Quraysh.[80] When al-Miqdad was looking for a spouse, he went to Abdur Rahman bin Awf, the richest companion, and asked to marry his daughter. Bin Awf became angry and refused to marry his daughter to al-Miqdad. He then went to the Prophet, and the Prophet could recognize in his face that he was troubled. He then informed the Prophet of bin Awf's refusal. The Prophet then arranged for him to marry Duba'ah, the daughter of his paternal uncle, who was described as being beautiful and intellectual. Thus the Prophet bestowed an honor upon al-Miqdad and arranged for him a spouse, which was superior to the one which he was refused.

Al-Miqdad passed away in al-Madinah at the age of 70 years old and was buried in al-Baq'i.[81]

---

80   Al-Baghawi, Mu'jam as-Sahabah, No. 2221
81   Ibn al-Jawzi, Sifah as-Safwah, Page 154

Salim Mawla Abi Hudhayfah

One of the pious teachers of the Qur'an among the companions was Salim bin Ma'qil.

Salim roots are from Istakhr, which is in the southern portion of modern day Iran. He is described as being black and was the first companion of the Prophet mentioned in Tanwir Al-Ghabash written by the prolific Hanbali scholar Abu al-Faraj bin Al-Jawzi.[82]

Salim embraced Islam in Makkah and was freed, becoming a client of Abu Hudhayfah. He was one who migrated to Al-Madinah for the sake of Allah. Abdullah bin Umar said that he was the most knowledgeable in the Qur'an of those who first migrated to Al-Madinah.

Later on in Al-Madinah, the Prophet ﷺ told the people that they should learn the Qur'an from four companions, those being Abdullah bin Mas'ud, Salim Mawla Abi Hudhayfah, Ubay bin Ka'ab and Mu'adh bin Jabal.

Salim accompanied Khalid bin Al-Walid, who was the general sent by the Prophet, to get allegiance from the Tribe of Jadhimah through Islam or have them pay taxes. Even though the men of Jadhimah declared Islam upon their visitation, Khalid began to kill them anyway. Salim reprimanded Khalid and listed off to him the crimes that he committed according to the sacred law. When word got back to the Prophet ﷺ regarding Khalid's unlawful killings, the Prophet proclaimed loudly, "Oh Allah! Surely I am

---

82   Bin Al-Jawzi, Tanwir Al-Ghabash fi Fadl as-Sudan wa al-Habash, Page 120

free of what Khalid has done!"[83] The Prophet said of Salim that "Allah loves the truth from his heart."

In Ghazwah Al-Yamamah, Salim urged the Muslims on by chanting, "Oh People of the Qur'an! Beautify the Qur'an with your deeds!" When the standard bearer Zayd bin al-Khattab was martyred, Salim lifted the standard. When his right hand was severed in the battle, he then continued by lifting it with his left hand. In this battle, Salim achieved martyrdom next to Abu Hudhayfah, his client.

---

83   Al-Bukhari, Sahih al-Bukhari, No. 4084

Ubadah bin as-Samit

One of the First Madani Muslims

One of the first Muslims to accept Islam among the People of Al-Madinah was Ubadah bin As-Samit.

Ubadah was born in al-Madinah and was from the Tribe of Khazraj.[84] He was described as being tall and very dark.[85]

Ubadah was one of those who took the pledge with the Prophet on the 2nd night of Aqabah before the Prophet and the Muslims in Makkah had migrated to Al-Madinah. He was one of the first 12 people of al-Madinah to accept Islam.[86] He later participated with the Prophet in all of the major campaigns including Badr, Uhud and Khandaq. He was also one of the scribes who wrote down the Qur'an.

During the government of Umar bin Al-Khattab when Egypt was conquered, Ubadah led a delegation to visit the Coptic leader al-Muqawqis. When Ubadah along with the rest of the delegation reached al-Muqawqis, the following conversation took place:

Al-Muqawqis: *Get this black man away from me, and bring me someone else to speak to me!*

The Muslims with Ubadah: *This black man is better than us in insight and knowledge. He is our leader, he is the best of us, and he has been appointed over us. We refer but to his speech and opinion. Certainly his command as the commander is upon us. And what he commands us, we do not differ from his insight and speech.*

---

84   Ibn Hibban, Tarikh as-Sahabah, Page 190

85   Al-Waqidi, Futuh as-Sham, Volume 1, Page 156

86   Adh-Dhahabi, Siyar Alam an-Nubala, Volume 1, Page 297

Al-Muqawqis: *How can you be pleased that a black man is better than you?! Rather he should be but the least among you.*

The Muslims: *Of course not! Even though he is a black man just like you see, he is best among us in status. He is the foremost among us in intellect and insight. Blackness is not despicable with us.*

Al-Muqawqis to Ubadah: Approach me, oh Black man, but speak to me gently for surely I am alarmed by your blackness! If you speak harshly with me, I will be more alarmed by you.

Ubadah then approached him: I heard what you said about me. Surely among my companions who I left behind are 1,000 men who are like me or blacker than I am, and even more terrifying for you to behold. If you saw them, you would be more alarmed by them than of me. I certainly know that I am not youthful. Nevertheless, I would not be scared if 100 men of my adversary, even if they all confronted me together. Thus the same is true for my companions. We hope and desire but struggle in the path of Allah and seek His pleasure. Our campaign is not against an enemy who wars against Allah for worldly gain or the accumulation of it. Rather that Allah Mighty and Sublime certainly made it lawful for us, and he made the booty for us permissible. None of us cares if we have qintars of gold nor if we possess a single dirham. All that we want from this world is something to eat to keep away hunger in the night and the day and cloth to wrap around ourselves. If none of us possesses more, that is enough. If he gets a qintar of gold, he spends it in obedience to Allah the Most High, and he will be content with this in his hand. It has reached him regarding what is in this life is that the pleasure of this world is not the real pleasure, nor is its luxury the real luxury. Pleasure and luxury are but in the hereafter. This is how Allah and his Prophet instructed us. He advised us that that our ambition in this world should be except to stave off hunger, cover our private parts, and be preoccupied and concerned in the pleasure of his Guardian, Sustainer and to struggle against His enemy.

Al-Muqawqis to the Egyptians around him: *Have you heard anything similar to this from a man before?! Surely his speech alarms me more than his appearance. Surely Allah has sent this man and his companions out to destroy the world! I think that their rule will but soon conquer all of the earth.*[87]

During the government of Uthman bin Affan, Ubadah spoke about problematic issues, which he witnessed in Syria. His speech upset the Governor of Syria Mu'awiyah bin Abi Sufyan. Mu'awiyah wrote to Uthman, "Surely Ubadah is the most troublesome in Syria to me and its people."[88] Ubadah was then sent to Uthman in which Ubadah responded to Mu'awiyah's accusations by saying, "The Prophet said, 'Torrential will be your affairs after me when men recognize what is wrong, but it will not be disliked for themselves what they recognize. So do not obey whoever disobeys nor send astray people from your Lord.'"[89]

Ubadah later moved to Jerusalem where he was buried at Al-Masjid Al-Aqsa during the government of Mu'awiyah bin Abi Sufyan.

87 Ibn Taghiri Birdi, An-Nujum az-Zahirah fi Muluk Misr wa al-Qahirah, Pages 18–19
88 Ibn Asakir, Tahdhib Tarikh, Volume 7, Pages 213 – 214
89 Al-Hakim, Al-Mustadrak ala As-Sahihayn, Hadith Number 5499

Eight Abyssinians who Migrated with Ja'far bin Abi Talib

There were two delegations of Muslims who fled Makkah to the Christian kingdom of Abyssinia due to the persecution of Quraysh. After Muslims were given protection in Abyssinia, there were eight Abyssinians who accepted Islam, then left Abyssinia to Al-Madinah with Ja'far bin Abi Talib, who was the cousin of Prophet Muhammad.

The names of those eight Abyssinians were:

Abrahah, Idris, Ashraf, Ayman, Bahir, Tammam, Tamim and Nafi'.

Tammam was a Jewish rabbi before accepting Islam.

Relating to Surah al-Qasas, ayah 52 which states, "Those to whom We gave the scripture before, they believe in it [Al-Qur'an]," al-Mawardi in his tafsir stated that one opinion is that this ayah is related to those eight Abyssinians who were from the People of the Book that accepted Islam.

Usamah bin Zayd
The Beloved Son of the Beloved

He is Usamah, the son of Zayd, the son of Harith, the son of Sharahil, the son of Abdul Uzza. His father was none other the only companion who is mentioned by name in the Quran. His father was at one time the adopted son of the Prophet Muhamad ﷺ until the ayah came down changing the custom of naming adopted children after their adopted parents (May Allah be pleased with him)

﴿وَإِذْ تَقُولُ لِلَّذِى أَنْعَمَ ٱللَّهُ عَلَيْهِ وَأَنْعَمْتَ عَلَيْهِ أَمْسِكْ عَلَيْكَ زَوْجَكَ وَٱتَّقِ ٱللَّهَ وَتُخْفِى فِى نَفْسِكَ مَا ٱللَّهُ مُبْدِيهِ وَتَخْشَى ٱلنَّاسَ وَٱللَّهُ أَحَقُّ أَن تَخْشَىٰهُ ۖ فَلَمَّا قَضَىٰ زَيْدٌ مِّنْهَا وَطَرًا زَوَّجْنَٰكَهَا لِكَىْ لَا يَكُونَ عَلَى ٱلْمُؤْمِنِينَ حَرَجٌ فِىٓ أَزْوَٰجِ أَدْعِيَآئِهِمْ إِذَا قَضَوْا مِنْهُنَّ وَطَرًا ۚ وَكَانَ أَمْرُ ٱللَّهِ مَفْعُولًا﴾

Usamah's mother was the illustrious Umm Ayman (May Allah be please with her) who was the wet nurse to the Prophet ﷺ and the one he ﷺ called: "My mother after my mother." Usamah was raised in the Prophetic household and was reared in piety and bravery. Ibn Jawzi mentions a story which displays the Prophet's ﷺ love for him and the sanctity of his person. He narrates that Abu Bakr ibn Abu Tahir al Bazzaz informed us on the authority of Hisham bin Urwah's father that the Messenger of Allah ﷺ delayed his return from Arafah to Makkah because he was waiting for Usamah bin Zayd. A flat nosed black youth appeared and the people of Yemen said to the Prophet ﷺ:"So you delayed us because of this boy? " The Prophet ﷺ responded:" Because of that the people of Yemen disbelieved. " I asked Yazid bin Harun what did he mean by his statement, "Because of that the people of Yemen disbelieved"?" He replied, "[He was referring to the people of Yemen's] apostasy during Abu Bakr's period, as a result of their lack of respect for the Prophet's ﷺ order. [90]

He tried his best to participate in the battle of Uhud at only 11 years old. He came onto the battlefield with a sword desiring to help defend the cause of Islam. He participated in the Battle of the Trench and was one of the few companions who never left the side of the Prophet ﷺ at the Battle of Hunain when most had abandoned the battlefield. He was also one of the couple of people to enter into the interior of the Kaaba along with the Prophet ﷺ on the day of the conquest of Makkah, along with Sayyidna Bilal (May Allah be pleased with him). Usamah is forever immortalized in the hadith literature as having killed a man in battle after the man uttered the testimony of faith. When the news of this reached the Holy Prophet ﷺ who asked Usamah why he killed the man, and Usamah responded that the man merely uttered the testimony of faith to save his life, the Prophet ﷺ famously responded:" Did you open his heart to check his sincerity." This incident has been related by Bukhari, Muslim and others. Usamah also has the honor of being the youngest person appointed by the Holy Prophet ﷺ as a general. Usamah was appointed to head the expedition to avenge the martyrdom of his illustrious father Zayd at the Battle of Mutah. Some of the companions objected to this and as a consequence, the Holy Prophet ﷺ mounted the minbar In his masjid and said:" Some people criticized Usamah's army command as they criticized his father's command before him. His father deserved to be the commander and so does Usamah. He is the most believed to me next to his

90   Abu'l Faraj ibn Jawzi, Tanwir-ul-Ghabas Fil Fadl Sudan wa'l Habash(Riyadh:Dar-ul-Sharif Lil Nashr wa'l Tawzee'a , 1997)pg. 132

father, I hope he is amongst the virtuous ones and I request you to treat him well." He was a mere 17 and commanded an army of Ansar and Muhajirin. At the death of the Holy Prophet ﷺ Abu Bakr was Usamah's permission to allow Umar bin Khattab to stay in Madina and help with the administration to which Usamah obliged. Usamah came back with no casualties and it was said that his army was the safest. Once during the reign of Umar ibn Khattab, Umar was distributing stipends for the senior companions and people of Badr etc. Umar's son Abdullah ibn Umar asked his father why was Usama getting double what he himself was getting and a stipend which was equal to the people of Badr. Umar responded:" The Messenger of Allah ﷺ loved him more than he ﷺ loved you, and he ﷺ loved his father more than he ﷺ loved our father." Usamah is buried in the graveyard of the companions in Jannah al-Baqi'

Aslam the Shepherd
Martyred before Making a Single Salah

There was a black companion who was martyred who did not know how to make Salah, never paid Zakah, nor fasted Ramadan during the Madani era. This companion was known as Aslam ar-Ra'i al-Aswad.

According al-Isabah compiled by ibn Hajar al-Asqalani, Aslam was from Abyssinian lineage and was a shepherd for Jewish people.[91] At Ghazwah Khaybar, Aslam came to the Prophet and accepted Islam. Without making a single prayer, he then joined those who fought at Khaybar and was martyred.

Upon hearing of Aslam's martyrdom, the Prophet 鸞 declared, "Surely he is with his wife, *al-hur al-'iyn.*"

---

91   Ibn Hajar, Al-Isbah, Volume 1, Page 216

Abu Bakra

His name was Nafi, but he is more widely known by the Kunya of Abu Bakra. When the Messenger of Allah ﷺ laid siege to al-Ta'if, his ﷺ herald announced that any slave who came out would be set free. A group of them came out, amongst them was Abu Bakra, he came down in a pulley (Bakra) and was subsequently known as "Abu Bakra."[92] He was counted amongst the freedmen of the Holy Prophet ﷺ. Abu Bakra and his son are amongst the many sahaba who Imam Bukhari and Muslim relates their hadiths. He stayed neutral in the dispute between Sayyidna Ali (Upon him be peace) and Sayyidna Aisha(A.S), he is known for not joining Sayyidna Aisha(upon her be peace) at the Battle of the Camel, when he recalled the hadith of the Prophet ﷺ:" The Nation which takes a woman as their leader shall not succeed."

Among the many beneficial hadiths he narrated from the Messenger of Allah ﷺ is:"The Prophet delivered to us a sermon on the Day of Nahr. He said, "Do you know what is the today?" We said, "Allah and His Apostle know better." He remained silent till we thought that he might give that day another name. He said, "Isn't it the Day of Nahr?" We said, "It is." He further asked, "Which month is this?" We said, "Allah and His Apostle know better." He remained silent till we thought that he might give it another name. He then said, "Isn't it the month of Dhul-Hijja?" We replied: "Yes! It is." He further asked, "What town is this?" We replied, "Allah and His Apostle know it better." He

---

92   Abu'l Faraj ibn Jawzi, *Tanwir-ul-Ghabas Fil Fadl Sudan wa'l Habash* (Riyadh:Dar-ul-Sharif Lil Nashr wa'l Tawzee'a , 1997) pgs. 133

remained silent till we thought that he might give it another name. He then said, "Isn't it the forbidden (Sacred) town (of Mecca)?" We said, "Yes. It is." He said, "No doubt, your blood and your properties are sacred to one another like the sanctity of this day of yours, in this month of yours, in this town of yours, till the day you meet your Lord. No doubt! Haven't I conveyed Allah's message to you? They said, "Yes." He said, "O Allah! Be witness. So it is incumbent upon those who are present to convey it (this information) to those who are absent because the informed one might comprehend it (what I have said) better than the present audience, who will convey it to him. Beware! Do not renegade (as) disbelievers after me by striking the necks (cutting the throats) of one another."

Yasar al-Aswad

Allah says in the 62nd verse of the 10th chapter of the Quran:" Surely the friends of Allah shall neither fear, nor shall they grieve." Allah also says in 251st verse of the 2nd chapter of the Quran:" If Allah had not checked one set of people by another, the earth would have indeed been full of corruption; but Allah is full of bounty to worlds." In Imam Qurtubi's tafsir to this verse, he mentions a narration from Abu Darda that states:" When Allah brought the institution of prophet hood to an end, He replaced them with men from the community of Muhammad ﷺ.[93]

These verses and other narrations such as what Imam Tabarani records in his Mu`jam al-awsat:"

Anas said that the Prophet said: "The earth will never lack forty men similar to the Friend of the Merciful [Prophet Ibrahim], and through them people receive rain and are given help. None of them dies except Allah substitutes another in his place,"

Qatada said: "We do not doubt that al-Hasan [al-Basri] is one of them,"

Ibn Hibban narrates it in al-Tarikh through Abu Hurayra ﷺ:

> The earth will never lack forty men similar to Ibrahim the Friend of the Merciful, and through whom you are helped, receive your sustenance, and receive rain," all point to a spiritual hierarchy which exist in the world of pious individuals whose prayers

---

93   Muhammad bin Ahmad Al-Qurtubi, *Jamia Al-Ahkam Al-Quran* (Beirut: Al-Resalah Publishers, 2006) pgs. 250-251

are accepted and integral for the good of mankind. Among these men was the companion of the Prophet 🐝 by the name of Yasar al-Aswad.

Ibn Jawzi and others narrate through various chains that Muhammad relays on the authority of Abu Hurayra who said: "I went into the Prophet's 🐝 mosque and he 🐝 said to me: 'O Abu Hurayra, in a moment a man will enter through this door, he is one of the seven with whom Allah will protect the earth.'[94]

Suddenly a mutilated Ethiopian man appeared through the door, carrying a jar of water on his head. The Messenger of Allah 🐝 said: 'this is him', welcome Yasar(three times).' Yasar used to sprinkle the mosque with water and sweep it out."

---

94   Abu'l Faraj ibn Jawzi, *Tanwir-ul-Ghabas Fil Fadl Sudan wa'l Habash* (Riyadh:Dar-ul-Sharif Lil Nashr wa'l Tawzee'a , 1997)pg. 142

Sa'ad al-Aswad

Internally Oppressed to Martyrdom

One of the black companions of the Prophet was Sa'ad al-Aswad as-Sulami.

Sa'ad was from the Ansar and suffered discrimination in Al-Madinah.

Due to an inferiority complex, Sa'ad asked the Prophet if he too could enter into Jannah because of his low position among the Muslims.[95] The Prophet replied to him that he was entitled to the same reward as other believers. Sa'ad then inquired that if he was an equal believer then why would none of the Arabs allow him to marry one of their daughters.

The Prophet then told Sa'ad to go to the home of 'Amr bin Wahb to ask him for his daughter for marriage. When Sa'ad told ibn Wahb that the Prophet sent him to request for his daughter for marriage, ibn Wahb became angry at the proposal. Ibn Wahb also stated to him that didn't he know that his daughter is known for her beauty! When ibn Wahb's daughter heard this, she told her father that she could not turn down a proposal that came at the suggestion of the Messenger of Allah!

Sa'ad was later martyred in a battle in which it is narrated that the Prophet wept over him while holding him in his lap.

---

95   Ibn al-Jawzi, Tanwir al-Ghabash, Page 136–137

Julaybib

One of the helpers of the Prophet ﷺ who is mentioned in a number of texts is the companion known as Julaybib (RA).

Julaybib accepted Islam in al-Madinah, thus is described as one of the men from the Helpers (*Ansar*). His lineage was unknown among the Arabs which made him an outcast. According to bin al-Jawzi, he was described as black (*aswad*).[96] The companion Abu Barzah (RA) also described him as short (*qasir*) and ugly (*damim*).[97]

Being that Julaybib had no tribal and family connections in al-Madinah as well as no wife, he spent more time in the company of the Prophet t han many of the other Ansar. In fact, the People of al-Madinah used to ridicule Julaybib and would not befriend him.

In narrations that are deemed sound, the Prophet proceeded to find a wife for the honorable Julaybib. When he went to the home of one of the Ansar, a father opened the door in which the Prophet told him that he came to him for a marriage proposal. The father immediately said yes thinking that his daughter would get the honor of being one of the Prophet's wives. The Prophet told him that he did not come for himself but was asking on behalf of Julaybib. The father then said that he was going to defer the decision to his wife.

When the wife of the Ansari came, the Prophet told her that he had a marriage proposal. The wife also became happy and said yes.

---

96   Bin al-Jawzi, Tanwir al-Ghabash fi Fadl as-Sudan wa al-Habash, Page 143
97   Bin al-Athir, Asad al-Ghabah, Volume 1, Page 348

Then the Prophet told her that he came on behalf of Julaybib. The wife then replied that she would not allow her daughter to marry a man like Julaybib!

Upon hearing noise, the daughter of the two came out and asked the reason for the Prophet coming to their home. The mother told the daughter that he came on behalf of Julaybib but that she was not accepting for her to marry him! The daughter replied, how can we turn down a proposal coming from the Messenger of Allah? She said to send Julaybib to her, for surely he will not bring ruin to her!

In Al-Asabah by ibn Hajar al-Asqalani, it is mentioned in reference to this event the application of surah 33, ayah 36, "It is not fitting for a believing man or woman that when Allah and His messenger decree a matter that they should have an opinion about it from their matter. And whoever disobeys Allah and His messenger surely is in clear error."[98] It is mentioned in several texts including Al-Musannaf by Abd ar-Razzaq in the Chapter of Compatibility in Marriage that the Prophet then performed the marriage between Julaybib and the lady.[99]

In a battle after the marriage, Julaybib achieved martyrdom. When the Prophet saw the martyred Julaybib, he said twice, "This [man] is from me, and I am from him." An-Ninawi said in his commentary of this narration in Sahih Muslim that the Prophet used exaggeration (*mubalaghah*) showing the importance of Julaybib as if Julaybib was a member of his ﷺ own klan such as when the Prophet said about Salman, who was Persian, "Salman is from us, the People of the Household (Ahl al-Bayt)."[100]

It is also narrated that the Prophet ﷺ personally dug the grave of Julaybib and placed him in the grave without washing him, signifying his status as a martyr.

---

98   Ibn Hajar al-Asqalani, Al-Isbah, Volume 2, Page 223
99   Abd ar-Razzaq As-San'ani, Al-Musannaf, No. 10086
100   An-Ninawi, Sharh an-Ninawi ala Muslim, No. 2472

Umm Zafar[101]

As shown throughout this series, the notion that Bilal ibn Rabah was the sole or rare representative of black people in Araba is utterly false. This is in regards to pre-Islamic Arabia and Islamic Arabia, as well as the larger Muslim world. Black or people of African origin were not the exception or novelties. Among the unsung Black companions of the Prophet ﷺ who was just blessed to receive the blessings of his ﷺ love and prayers was Umm Zafar. Imams Bukhari and Muslim narrated on the authority of Ibn Abu Rabah that he said:" Ibn Abbas ﷺ said: 'Do you want me to show you a woman from paradise?' I responded, yes. He then said: "This black woman came to the Messenger of Allah ﷺ and said: 'I suffer from epileptic fits from which I expose myself. Pray to Allah for me.' He ﷺ said: 'If you are patient, then you will be rewarded with paradise. If you wish, I can pray to Allah to cure you.' She said: 'I will be patient, but in my fits I expose myself, so pray to Allah that I don't expose myself anymore.' So he prayed for her."

---

101   Abu'l Faraj ibn Jawzi, Tanwir-ul-Ghabas Fil Fadl Sudan wa'l Habash (Riyadh: Dar-ul-Sharif Lil Nashr wa'l Tawzee'a , 1997)pg. 150

Abu Niyzar and Nasr
Devotees to the Prophetic Household

Abu Niyzar was a companion of the Prophet from Abyssinian heritage. According to ibn Hajr al-Asqalani and others, he was a son of Annajashi, the Abyssinian emperor who embraced Islam.[102]

Abu Niyzar embraced Islam at a young age then migrated from Abyssinia to al-Madinah. His father migrated from Abyssinia but died before reaching the Prophet. Once reaching al-Madinah, Abu Niyzar loyally served the Prophet. After the passing of the Prophet, he attached himself to serving Fatimah Az-Zahra then serving one of her son's after her passing away.

Ibn Hajar and others narrate that Abu Niyzar was the caretaker of a garden owned by the Prophetic Household named al-Bughayghah upon the instruction of Imam Ali. From it one day, Abu Niyzar prepared a meal in which Imam Ali ate and drank from it. Imam Ali then stated that a condition of the garden was that it be an endowment and what came forth from it would provide for the needy and wayfarers in al-Madinah, unless Imam al-Hasan bin Ali or Imam al-Husayn bin Ali needed to sell it.

After the martyrdom of Imam Ali, Imam al-Husayn was in need of repaying a debt, and this news reached Mu'awiyah bin Abi Sufyan. Mu'awiyah then offered Abu Niyzar a large sum of money to sell the garden, but was refused because it was to remain as an endowment for the poor in al-Madinah.

Once Mu'awiyah died and his son Yazid came into power, Abu Niyzar's son Nasr refused to give allegiance to Yazid. Nasr

---

102   Ibn Hajar al-Asqalani, *Al-Isabah*, Vol. 7, Page 323

like his father remained a devotee to the Prophetic Household. He accompanied Imam al-Husayn from al-Madinah to Makkah then to Karbala where he achieved martyrdom with his imam.[103]

---

103   Al-Mubarrid, *Al-Kamal fi al-Lughah wa al-Adab*, Vol. 3, Pages 207–208

Ata ibn Abi Rabah[104]

Amongst the outstanding people of knowledge from the blessed generation of the tabieen, who were black was Ata ibn Abi Rabah. Ata was a citadel of knowledge whose intercession was sought and request were obeyed by the rulers. He studied under the likes of Ibn Umar, Abu Sa'id, Abu Hurayra, Ibn Abbas and others. He distinguished himself with knowledge and piety. Ismail Ahmad As-Samarqandi has related on the authority of Imam Ahmad ibn Hanbal who said;" Knowledge is a treasure which God bestows upon whom He loves. Ata ibn Abi Rabah was an Abyssinian."

Muhammad ibn Al-Baqi said that Ahmad ibn Muhammad used to attend the classes on Quranic exegesis at the Holy Kaaba given by Ibn Abbas After him they were given by Ata. Muhammad ibn Abi Tahir has related on the authority of Salma bin Kuhayl that he said:" I never knew anyone who sought knowledge for the sake of God except for three: Ata, Ta'us and Mujahid." Ismail bin Ahmad relates on the authority of Ismail bin Ummaya that he said:" Ata was a quiet man, but whenever he spoke it was if he was being inspired."

Abu Mansur Muhammad relays an interesting story about Ata's exhortation to Hisham ibn Abdul Malik. He says that's Uthman bin Ata Al-Khurasani said:" I accompanied on a visit to Hisham. As we approached, a black man with dirty clothes, a dirty cloak and a dirty cap appeared on a camel. I laughed and said to my father who is this Bedouin? (This is interesting as it

---

104   Abu'l Faraj ibn Jawzi, *Tanwir-ul-Ghabas Fil Fadl Sudan wa'l Habash* (Riyadh: Dar-ul-Sharif Lil Nashr wa'l Tawzee'a , 1997) pgs. 153-154

shows that being black in tone was so common amongst the Arabs that the narrator thought that Ata was a Bedouin Arab) He said (his father) 'be quiet, for this is the leader of the jurist of the Hijaz.' This is Ata ibn Abi Rabah. When he drew near to us my father got down off of his mule and Ata off of his camel and they exchanged pleasantries. They then mounted again and proceeded to Hisham's place. When my father returned I asked him what had happened between the two. He replied:' when Hisham was informed that Ata had come to see him, he requested that Ata be allowed in. By Allah, without him (Ata) I would not have been able to see Hisham. When Hisham saw him he said, welcome, welcome, and pulled him so close that their knees were touching.

They were some nobles of Quraish with Hisham who were talking but then they became quiet. Hisham said. What are your needs Abu Muhammad? Ata responded:' O commander of the faithful, I am asking for sustenance for the people of Makkah and Madina, the people of God, and the neighbors of the Messenger of God 🐝. Hisham responded, certainly, O servant arrange for a year's provision and sustenance for the people of Makkah and Madina.' He asked, do you have any other request O Abu Muhammad? [Ata] Yes, O Commander of the Faihful, I am asking that the people of the Hijaz and Nejd be given their entitlements. These people are the originators and masters of the Arabs. He [Hisham] said:' Certainly, O servant, arrange that they be given their entitlements.

Do you have any requests other than these O Abu Muhammad?' Yes [Ata]' O Commander of the Faithful, the people of Thaghur, they have been defending your territories and fighting your enemies, you used to give them a stipend. If they were to perish then you would be invaded.'

[Hisham]' Certainly, O Servant arrange that they be given a stipend.'

Do you have any requests other than these O Abu Muhammad? Ata said:, ' Yes O Commander of the Faithful, Do not let the young and the old amongst your servants suffer and be made to do more than they can bear.' [Hisham] '

Certainly, O servant arrange that they not be asked to do more than what the can bear.' [Ata] said:' Yes, O Commander of the Faithful, Fear God within yourself for you were created alone, and you will die alone, you will be resurrected alone, you will called to account alone. I swear by God that none of these people will be around you will be with you.' Hisham broke down. Ata stood up. When we reached the door, a man came after Ata with a bag. I don't know whether it was dinars or dirhams. The man said:' The Commander of the Faithful asked me to give you this', Ata said:' I do not ask any reward from you. My reward is from God, the Lord of the worlds.' Then Ata went out without a sip of water."

Ibrahim bin Mahdi
The Black Caliph

He is Ibrahim the son of Mahdi, the son of Mansur the son of Muhammad the son of Ali the son of Abdullah the son of Abbas who was the uncle of the Prophet (Peace of God be upon him). He was recognized as the fourth Abbasid caliph for a period. His mother was an Afro-Iranian princess named Shikla or Shakla. The historian Khallikan described the prince as "very black." He was very learned, an excellent musician as well as a poet. He was acknowledged as Caliph.

He was chosen to be the caliph because when Al-Ma'mun had designated Ali Ridha to succeed him, the Bani Abbas revolted. The Bani Abbas proclaimed: "We will not allow the issue of succession to be taken out of our hands." They then chose Ibrahim as their candidate and began to read the Friday sermon in his name.[105] His popularity in Kufa was overwhelming, but when Ali Ridha died and Al- Ma'mun returned to Kufa then Ibrahim's popularity declined and the people deserted him. He went into hiding and remained so for 6 years, 4 months and 2 days. He grew tired of being in hiding and wrote to Al-Ma'mun saying: "O Commander of the Faithful, you have a definite case of revenge against me, but to forego revenge would be better. Whoever allows himself to be deceived by the power that he has been given should be sure of the consequences in this life. God has

---

105   Abu'l Faraj ibn Jawzi, *Tanwir-ul-Ghabas Fil Fadl Sudan wa'l Habash* (Riyadh:Dar-ul-Sharif Lil Nashr wa'l Tawzee'a , 1997) pg. 160

ranked the Commander of the Faithful above those who deserve forgiveness, just as He has ranked him above the sinners. If the Commander chooses to forgive, then it is a favor from him. If he chooses to punish then that is also within his right to do so."

Al-Mamun examined the case before him and said: "Power to revenge dispels anger, and honesty is sufficient repentance." Then Ibrahim came to him and said: "If I am a sinner then I am responsible for my mistakes, do not blame yourself too much. Say as Yusuf said to Yacub's sons when they came to him: "No reproach shall be uttered against you today.' He died in 839 C.E.

Muhammad ibn Hanifiyah

He is Muhammad, the son of Amir-ul-Mumineen Ali ibn Abi Talib 👤 is known in antiquity as "Ibn Hanifiyah" because of his mother. There is a difference of opinion as to where she was a black lady of Sind origin[106] or a Khalah bint Jafar from Banu Hanifa. Ibn Jawzi says that she was a black woman of Sind origin. The two different narrations agree that his mother was captured during the Apostasy Wars, particularly from the people of Yamamah. As we have already seen, Imam Ali was described as black by a plethora of historians.

According to the narrations which say that she was Khala bint Jafar, it was said that her tribe petitioned Imam Ali to free her and save her from the stain of slavery. He married her and set her free. Their son Muhammad participated in the battles of Jamal and Siffin. He was willing to sacrifice himself so that the sons of Fatima 👤 would not be cut down. He later advised his older brother Imam Hussain 👤 to not go to Kufa to accept the bayah of the people there. He advised the Imam to go to Yemen, where he could raise an army. After the catastrophe of Karbala, Imam Ali bin Hussain 👤 retired from politics and Muhammad ibn Hanifiya became the most apparent head of the Alid clan of Bani Hashim. The Kaysanite Shia claimed that the divine Imamate passed from Ali, then Hassan, then Hussain and then Muhammad Hanifiya.

---

106 Abu'l Faraj ibn Jawzi, *Tanwir-ul-Ghabas Fil Fadl Sudan wa'l Habash* (Riyadh: Dar-ul-Sharif Lil Nashr wa'l Tawzee'a , 1997)pg.228

Al-Mukhtar Thaqafi later led his famous rebellion in the name of Muhammad ibn Hanifiah. Muhammad would lead his own delegation of followers on the pilgrimage. He later stopped fighting and gave allegiance to Abdul Malik and retired in Madinah where he died around 700 AD/ 81 Hijrah. Some of his followers said that that he was banished to Mount Radwa because of his agreement to a détente with Abdul-Malik. News of his death came as a shock to his followers who spread the myth that he was not dead and would indeed return.

Sa'id ibn Jubair

He is Abu Muhammad Sa'id ibn Jubair. He was born in Kufa in the 30ᵗʰ year of the hijra, during the reign of Imam Hassan ibn Abi Talib ﷺ. Imam Dhahabi describes him as being "black in color." Sa'id was from amongst the most learned and ascetic of the tabieen. He was a doyen of piety and enjoys universal acclaim and praise from both Sunni and Shia scholars.

Shaykh Al-Tusi counted him from amongst the companions of Imam Zain-ul-Abidin. Ibn Hajar Asqalani said about him: "....He narrated hadiths from Ibn Abbas, Ibn Al-Zubair, Ibn Umar, Ibn Maqal, Uday Ibn Hatem, Abi Masood Al-Ansary, Abi Saeed Al-Khudari, Abu Hurayra, Abu Musa Al-Asha'ari, Al-Dahak Ibn Qais Al-Fehri, Anas, Amro Ibn Maymoon, Abi Abdur-Rahman Al-Sulami and lady A'isha..... Ibn Abi Mughira said that when people of Kufa visit Ibn Abbas they used to ask him for Fatwa, he used to say them: "Isn't Sa'id Ibn Jubair among you?".... Amro Ibn Maymun said that his father said that Sa'id Ibn Jubair passed away and everyone on the earth attained his knowledge... Abu Al-Qasem Al-Tabari said: "He is a reliable Imam and hujjah(proof) on Muslims".....Ibn Hibban said: "He was jurist, worshiper, righteous and pious"[107]

Sa'id was a reliable narrator who Imam Bukhari relays some 147 narrations from. Imam Muslim narrates 78 traditions from him in his Sahih collection. He was one of the students of Ibn Abbas in Quranic exegesis. Being from the Makkan scholars of exegesis, his opinions were relied upon in the east and west.

---

107   *Tahdhib al-Tahdhib* Volume 4 No. 14

During the reign of the Umayyad Caliph Al-Walid, a delegation of disgruntled mawali came to Hasan Al-Basri in order to get his approval for a rebellion against the Ummayads and their governor Al-Hajjaj bin Yusuf. The delegation was headed by Abdur-Rahman ibn Ash'ath. They began to question Hasan: " What do you say about one who spills the sacred blood of the Muslims and violates the holy precincts and murders the companions of the Prophet ﷺ ? Hassan: I don't think that you should fight him. If he is oppressive and you don't deserve him then ask Allah to remove him. But know that if he is placed over you as a result of your sins then you will never be able to remove him by your swords. The delegation left and went out to fight Hajjaj and the forces of Abdul Malik bin Marwan. This battle is known in posterity as the Battle of the Monastery of Skulls (Dayr al-Jamajim).

In the 82ⁿᵈ year of the hijra (701 C.E.)[108] Sa'id ibn Jubair and Kumayl bin Ziyad headed a battalion known as the "Battalion of the Quran Reciters" against the Umayyad army. Although they had superior numbers and initially forced Abdul Malik to the negotiating table, they were later routed. Ibn Jubair escaped the battle field and fled to the outskirts of Makkah.

He secretly enter Makkah twice a year for Hajj and Umrah. He would also clandestinely enter Kufa in order to answer perplexing legal questions for the people of Kufa. Sa'id was finally subsequently captured and brought before Al-Hajjaj after Khalid Abdullah Al-Qasri, the governor of Makkah, threatening the people of Makkah that he would kill anyone harboring Sa'id. This is a recounting of the final moments of Sa'id's life:

Sa'īd ibn Jubair entered upon al-Hajjāj, who asked his name (and he knew his name well):

Sa'īd: Sa'īd bin Jubair. Al-Hajjaj: Nay, you are Shaqiy bin Kusayr. (Sa'id means happy and Shaqiy means unhappy; Jubair means one who splints broken bones and Kusayr means one who breaks them.) Sa'īd: My mother knew better when she named me. Al-Hajjāj: You are wretched (*shaqayta*) and your mother is wretched" (*shaqiyat*). Then he told him: "By Allah, I will replace your dunya with a blazing Fire. Sa'īd: If I knew you could do it, I would take you as a God. Al-Hajjāj: I have gold and wealth.

108   Hawting, G.R. (2000). The First Dynasty of Islam: The Umayyad Caliphate AD 661–750 (2nd Edition). London and New York: Routledge. pp. 68–69

Bags of gold and silver were brought and spread before Sa'īd bin Jubair in order to try him.

Sa'īd: O Hajjāj, if you gathered it to be seen and heard in showing off, and to use it to avert others from the way of Allah, then by Allah, it will not avail you against Him in any way. Saying this, he aligned himself towards Qiblah. Al-Hajjāj: Take him and turn him to other than the Qiblah. By Allah, O Sa'īd bin Jubair, I will kill you with a killing with which I have not killed any of the people. Sa'īd: O Hajjāj choose for yourself whatever killing you want, by Allah you will not kill me with a killing except that Allah will kill you with a like of it, so choose for yourself whatever killing you like. Al-Hajjāj: Turn him to other than the Qiblah. Sa'īd: Wherever you [might] turn, there is the Face of Allah.[109] Al-Hajjāj: Put him under the earth. Sa'īd: From it (the earth) We created you, and into it We will return you, and from it We will extract you another time.[110]

Al-Hajjāj was enraged and ordered that Sa'id be decapitated. At that moment, Sa'id looked at the sky and said: Allah, don't forgive him for persecuting me! Punish him for my blood! And make me the last person he kills of Muhammad's nation! Immediately, the headsman beheaded him. The head fell to the ground and said: There's no god but Allah!

Al-Hajjāj began looking at the continuous flowing of the blood. He was astonished to see the plentiful blood. So, he asked the coroner about it and the coroner said: All those you killed were afraid. Their blood stopped in their veins. So, there was no bleeding. But Sa'id was not afraid. His heart was beating normally. Sa'īd was martyred in the month of Sha'bān, 95 AH (ca. May 714) at the age of 49. Al-Hajjāj is reported to have went insane. He constantly had nightmares and would wake up yelling: Why have I killed Sa'id ibn Jubair? He died 15 days later.

---

109   Qur'an, 2:115
110   Qur'an, 20:55

Noble and Notable Arabs of Ethiopian Mothers

As previously discussed in the section on the hajins and the nuanced definition on just what an Arab was in antiquity, it is prudent to mention here a number of other noble and notable Arabs who were the offspring of Ethiopian women. These individuals were considered Arab and from the gentry of Arab society. Amongst them were: Nadla bin Hasham bin Abdil Manaf bin Qusay.[111] Nadla was the great uncle of the Prophet Muhammad ﷺ, Nufail bin Abdil Uzza Al-Adawi.

This Nufail was the grandfather of the companion of the Prophet Muhammad ﷺ, Umar bin Khattab, who was also the second of the rightly guided caliphs. Nufail once arbitrated a dispute between Abdul Muttalib, the grandfather of the Prophet Muhammad ﷺ, and Harab bin Ummayah in regards to the custodianship of the Holy Ka'abah in Makkah. Nufail gave his decision in favor of Abdul Muttalib. He said to Harab:" Why do you pick a quarrel with a person who is taller than you in stature, more imposing in appearance, more refined in intellect, one whose progeny outnumbers yours, and one whose generosity outshines yours? Do not construe this as a disparagement of any of your fine accolades which I do appreciate. You are gentle as a lamb, and renowned throughout Arabia for your voice, and you are an invaluable asset to you tribe."

---

111   Abu'l Faraj ibn Jawzi, Tanwir-ul-Ghabas Fil Fadl Sudan wa'l Habash(Riyadh:Dar-ul-Sharif Lil Nashr wa'l Tawzee'a ,p 246.

A list of other notable Arabs with Ethiopian mothers includes:

- Khattab bin Nufail, this was the father of Umar bin Khattab
- Umru bin Rabia bin Habib
- Harith bin Abi Rabia al-Makhzumi
- Uthman bin Huwarith bin Assad bin Abdul Uzza
- Safwan bin Ummayah bin Khalf Al-Jumh
- Hisham bin Uqba bin Abi Mu'eeth
- Malik bin Abdullah bin Jad'an,[112]
- Ubaidullah bin Abdullah bin Abi Malkia
- Musafih bin Iyyad bin Sakhr Al-Taimi
- Amr bin Al-As bin Wa'il (Al-Sahmi)[113]
- Amr bin Nawful bin Abdul Manaf
- Malik bin Hassan bin Amr bin Lu'i
- Abdullah bin Qais bin Abdullah bin Zubair
- Samra bin Habib bin Abd Shams
- Abdullah bin Zam'a from Bani Amr bin Lu'i
- Amr bin Hasis bin Ka'ab bin Lu'i
- Abdullah bin Abdullah bin Amr bin Kareez
- Muhammad Taqi bin Ali bin Musa bin Jafar bin Muhammad Baqir bin Ali also known as "Zainul-Abidin", bin Hussain, bin Ali bin Abi Talib,[114]
- Jafar bin Ismai'il bin Musa bin Jafar
- Ubaidullah bin Hamza bin Musa bin Jafar
- Muhammad and Jafar are the sons of Ibrahim bin Hassan bin Hassan bin Ali bin Abi Talib
- Sulaiman bin Hassan from Bani Aqil bin Abi Talib
- Muhammad bin Dawud bin Muhammad from Bani Hassan bin Ali bin Ai Talib

---

112   Malik's father Abdullah bin Jad'an hosted the famed "Hilf-ul-Fudul", which guaranteed the rights of those who didn't belong to powerful Makkan families and established a common human rights pact.

113   As found in Suyuti's "Rafa Shan al-Habshan"

114   Imam Muhammad and others of his lineage will be discussed in the upcoming "Black Imams of Ahl Bait"

- Ahmad bin Abdul Malik bin Uthman bin Affan
- Ahmad bin Muhammad bin Salih Al-Makhzumi
- Abbas bin Mutasim (Abbassid caliph)
- Hiba Allah bin Ibrahim bin Mahdi
- Muhammad bin Abdullah bin Ishaq al-Mahdi
- Isa and Jafar the sons of Jafar Mansur (Abbassid Caliph)
- Abbas bin Muhammad bin Ali bin Abdullah ibn Abbas
- Abdul Wahab bin Ibrahim bin Muhammad.

The aforementioned persons were listed by as-Suyuti who narrates from Ibn Jawzi in his "Raising the affair of the Ethiopians". He also comments that Ibn Jawzi mentioned even more and included those from the pre-Islamic era of *jahilia*. Suyuti kept his list to the era of Islam with a concentration on those who were Muslim. Of those he mentioned who were companions were Safwan bin Ummayah bin Khalf al-Jamhi, and Amr bin al-Aas. Of the subsequent generations who were Muslim were: Abdullah bin Qais bin Abdullah bin Zubair, Abdullah bin Aamir bin Kareez, Muhammad bin Ali bin Musa, bin Jafar as-Sadiq bin Muhammad Baqir bin Ali (Zain-ul-Abidin), bin Hussain, Jafar bin Ismai bin Musa bin Jafar, Ubaidullah bin Musa bin Jafar, Ibrahim bin Hassan Muthanna bin Hassan, Sulaiman bin Hassan bin Aqil bin Abi Talib, Yala bin Walid bin Uqba bin Abi Mu'it, Abbas bin Muhammad bin Ali bin Abdullah bin Abbas, Isa and Jafar, the sons of Abi Jafar al-Mansur, Hiba'llah bin Ibrahim bin Mahdi, and Abbas bin Mu'tasim.

Also of note here is the Abbassid caliph Muqtadir li-Amr-llah. He wasn't mentioned by Ibn Jawzi, but as-Suyuti mentions him on page 20 of his "Azhar Arush fi Akbar ul Hubush."

Conclusion

"Blackness" as a term has carried varying meanings in different eras among diverse nations. As a consequence to historical trends, any discussion of Blackness with Muslims in this current era unfortunately carries with it a level of controversy. The mental conditioning of Muslims in the past century through educational and popular cultural influences from the West which systematically privileged Whiteness cannot be understated. Though Muslims have never been post-tribalism, the implicit biases existing among many Muslims has lead many to view Whiteness as more beautiful, Blackness as being less attractive, less Arab thus less Muslim and less authoritative in the classic development of Islamic scholastic thought.

It was important for us to provide evidence from early Islamic texts to deal with the issues of Blackness and Arabness, in particular to show how these two frames were not viewed as mutually exclusive in the early generations of Muslims. Moreover it was incumbent upon us to bring readers beyond generic descriptive terminology as many commonly misunderstand to a more nuanced understanding based upon the semantics of the Arabic language. This was a necessary endeavor embarked upon in this book before providing brief biographical information of the personalities therein. Some of these nobles, of course, were commonly known to the generality already while others were unknown except by scholars.

This humble publication sought to unveil some of those hidden nobles to be known to the general Muslim community. In sha Allah, this is but the first in a series of other publications that will delve into greater depth of the historical relationship between Africa and the Arabian Peninsula and figures and movements related to Blackness in the early centuries of Islamic civilization.

Bibliography

Several of the source authors noted herein are of Arabic or Islamic persuasion, their names being a reflection of their ethnicity or heritage. Due to differences in phonetics between the Arabic language and English, as well as those found the morphology and grammatical constructions between to two languages, in order to facilitate referencing to bibliography, certain mechanisms have been put into place.

In the Arabic language, it is common place for some names, especially, but not exclusively sir names, that these will preceded with a definite article, often expressed and transliterated to "Al", or sometimes, "Ad-", "Adh-", "As-", "Ash-", "At-", "Az-". In the case of the latter six examples, the single letter or digraph following the "A" in these articles phonotically matches the first letter or digraph of the base noun/propoer noun. This is done in the Arabic in order to facilitate ease in the transition from the article to the base noun simliar to "un" and "um" articles in Spanish. For example, and name the starts with the "S" sound, such as Samman would utilize the article "As-", rendering it to "As-Samman"; and the name Shafi'i would be preceded by the article "Ash-", so the it would read "Ash-Shafi'i. Aside from the aforementioned examples given, all over definite articles in Arabic are, by default, pronounced and transliterated as "Al-".

In order to facilitate referencing this bibliography, the definite article in most cases, though indicated, have otherwise been phonetically eliminated for the sake of alphabetization. Here, the articles are presented in small case form and contained within parentheses. However wherever it may occur that a particular Muslim/Arab personality is so well established and recognized that omitting the article might likely result in confusion, the article is maintained as part of the name. In such cases, the name will be classified with the "A" group each time.

It is likewise important to note that the common Arab/Semitic prefix "Ibn" (son/son of) may, in rare cases, be eliminated provided use of this designation is not commonly associated with the person being referenced and the reader should bypass this and make their reference by way of the first letter(s) of the sir name. In most cases here, however, "Ibn" is assumed to be an established part of the name and then the reader would search the "I" portion of the bibliography in order to reference it.

Abi Talib, Ali (bin); "Diwan al-Imam Ali bin Abi Talib"; Page 114

Activities of Dr. Ernst Schaefer, OI – Final Interrogation Report (OI-FIR) No. 32, Secret – United States Forces European Theater Military Intelligence Service Center APO 757, The; February 12, 1946, Page 4.

Ahlwardt, Wilhelm; "The Diwans of the Six Ancient Arabic Poets Ennabigha, 'Antarah Tharafa, Zuhair, 'Alqama, and Imrul Qais"; (London 1870), p 42. See Encyclopedia of Islam, 2d., s.v. "Antarah."

Ali, Zayd (bin); "Musnad al-Imam Zayd"; Pages 395–396

Al-Hakim; "Al-Mustadrakala as-Sahihayn"; Hadith number 5650(al-) Asqalani, Ibn Hajar; "Al-Isbah"; Volume 2, Page 223

(al-)Asqalani, Ibn Hajar; "Al-Isabah"; Vol. 7, Page 323

Al-Qadi, an-Nu'man; "Sharh Al-Akhbar"; Juz 2, Page 427

Al-Qurtubi, Muhammad bin Ahmad; "Jamia Al-Ahkam Al-Quran"; Beirut: Al-Risalah Publishers, 2006, Pages 250-251

(al-)Baghawi; "Mu'jam as-Sahabah"; No. 2221

(al-)Baghdadi, Al-Khatib; "Tarikh al-Baghdadi"; Juz 1, Page 145

(al-)Bukhari; "Sahih al-Bukhari"; Hadith Number 3522

Birdi, Ibn Taghiri; "An-Nujum az-Zahirah fi Muluk Misr wa al-Qahi-rah"; Pages 18–19

Blumenbach, Johan Freidrich; "The Anthropological Treatises of Johan Friedrich Blumenbach; The Natural Varieties of Mankind"; London: The Anthropological Society, 1865, Page265

Bowersock, Glen W.; "The Rise and fall of a Jewish Kingdom in Arabia, Institute Journal of Institute of Advanced Study"; Fall 2011 Issue

(al-)Bukhari; "Sahih al-Bukhari"; No. 4084

Collins, Adrian and Gobineau, Arthur; "The Inequality of Human Races"; New York: G.P. Putman's Sons. 1915, Page 212.

(al-)Dhahabī, Muḥammad b. Aḥmad b. 'Uthmān; "Siyar al-A'lām al-Nubalā'"; Beirut: Mu'assasa al-Risāla, 1981

(adh-)Dhahabi; "Tarikh al-Islam"; Juz 3, Page 624

(adh-)Dhahabi; "Siyar Alam an-Nubala"; Volume 1, Page 297

http://discovermagazine.com/1994/nov/thegeometerofrac441

Dubois, W.E.B; "The Souls of Black Folks. New York: Simon and Schuster Paperbacks"; 2009 edition, Page 3

Embassy of the Republic of Korea to the Republic of South Africa, The; http://zaf.mofa.go.kr/english/af/zaf/bilateral/bilateral/index.jsp

Encyclopedia Britannica s.v. Arabian Desert. Britannica Online at http://www.britannica.com/EBchecked/topic/31610/Arabian-Desert. Accessed February 12, 2009.

Garner, Steve; "Racisms: An Introduction. London"; SAGE Publications Ltd, 2010, Page 79

Collins, Adrian and Gobineau, Arthur; "The Inequality of Human Races"; New York: G.P. Putman's Sons. 1915, Page 212.

Goldenberg, David M.; "The Curse of Ham: Race and Slavery in Judaism, Christianity, and Islam"; Princeton and Oxford: Princeton University Press, 2003, Page 197

Haas, Christopher; "Geopolitics and Georgian Identity in Late Antiquity: The Dangerous World of Vakhtang Gorgasali," in Tamar Nutsubidze, Cornelia B. Horn, Basil Lourié (eds.), Georgian Christian Thought and Its Cultural Context, BRILL Pages 29-44, 36-39 (al-)Hasani, Ibn ash-Shajari; "Ma Ittifaqa Lafzuhu wa Ikhtilaf Ma'nah"; Volume 1, Page 5

Hawting, G.R.; (2000) "The First Dynasty of Islam: The Umayyad Caliphate AD 661–750"; (2nd Edition); London and New York: Routledge; Pages 68–69

(Ibn) Hishām, 'Abd Al-Malik; Al-Sīra Al-Nabawiya; Beirut: Mu'assasa al-Ma'ārif, 2004, Page 205.

Ibn Asakir; "Tahdhib Tarikh"; Volume 7, Pages 213 – 214

Ibn al-Athir; "Asad al-Ghabah"; Volume 1, Page 348

Ibn Hajr; "Al-Isbah"; Volume 8, Page 88

Ibn Hajar; "Al-Isbah"; Volume 1, Page 216

Ibn Hibban; "Tarikh as-Sahabah"; Page 60

Ibn Hibban; "Tarikh as-Sahabah"; Page 230

Ibn Hibban; "Tarikh as-Sahabah"; Page 190

Ibn al-Jawzi; "Manaqib al-Imam Ahmad bin Hanbal"; Page 163

Ibn al-Jawzi; "Sifwah as-Safwah"; Page 122

Ibn al-Jawzi; "Sifah as-Safwah"; Page 303

Ibn al-Jawzi; "Tanwir al-Ghabash"; Page 131

Ibn al-Jawzi; "Sifah as-Safwah"; Page 153

Ibn al-Jawzi; "Sifah as-Safwah"; Page 154

Ibn Al-Jawzi; "Tanwir Al-Ghabash fi Fadl as-Sudan wa al-Habash"; Page 120

Ibn Jawzi, Abu'l Faraj; "Tanwir-ul-Ghabas Fil Fadl Sudan wa'l Habash"; Riyadh: Dar-ul-Sharif Lil Nashr wa'l Tawzee'a , 1997, Pages 133

Ibn al-Jawzi; "Tanwir al-Ghabash"; Page 136–137

Ibn al-Jawzi; "Tanwir al-Ghabash fi Fadl as-Sudan wa al-Habash"; Page 143

Ibn Jawzi, Abu'l Faraj; "Tanwir-ul-Ghabas Fil Fadl Sudan wa'l Habash"; Riyadh: Dar-ul-Sharif Lil Nashr wa'l Tawzee'a, 1997, Page 150

Ibn Jawzi, Abu'l Faraj; "Tanwir-ul-Ghabas Fil Fadl Sudan wa'l Habash"; Riyadh: Dar-ul-Sharif Lil Nashr wa'l Tawzee'a , 1997, Pages 153-154

Ibn Jawzi, Abu'l Faraj; "Tanwir-ul-Ghabas Fil Fadl Sudan wa'l Habash" Riyadh: Dar-ul-Sharif Lil Nashr wa'l Tawzee'a , 1997; Page 160

Ibn Jawzi, Abu'l Faraj; "Tanwir-ul-Ghabas Fil Fadl Sudan wa'l Habash"; Riyadh: Dar-ul-Sharif Lil Nashr wa'l Tawzee'a, 1997; Page 228

Ibn Jawzi, Abu'l Faraj; "Tanwir-ul-Ghabas Fil Fadl Sudan wa'l Habash"; Riyadh: Dar-ul-Sharif Lil Nashr wa'l Tawzee'a; Page 246

Ibn Kathir, Al-Bidayah wa an-Nihayah, 5/8

Ibn Sa'ad; "At-Tabaqat al-Kubra"; Number 10345

Ibn Sa'ad; "At-Tabaqat al-Kubra"; Volume 4, Page 432

Ibn Shar, Ashub; "Manaqib Aali Abi Talib"; Juz 3, Page 91

Malik's father, Abdullah bin Jad'an, hosted the famed "Hilf-ul-Fudul", which guaranteed the rights of those who didn't belong to powerful Makkan families and established a common human rights pact

(al-)Majlisi; "Bihar al-Anwar"; Juz 35, Page 2

Mazrui, Ali A.; "Euro-Jews and Afro-Arabs, The Great Semitic Divergence in World History"; (Lanham: University Press of America, 2008) 140

(al-) Mizzi; "Tahdhib al-Kamal"; Juz 20, Page 480

(al-)Mubarrid; "Al-Kamal fi al-Lughah wa al-Adab"; Vol. 3, Pages 207–208

(al-)Mu'ayyidi, Ibn Mansur; "At-Tuhf Sharh az-Zalaf"; Page 24

Musa, Ali (bin); "Sahifah al-Imam ar-Rida"; Page 70

Muslim; "Sahih Muslim"; Number 2453

(al-)Nawawī, Yaḥya b. Sharaf; "Ṣaḥīḥ Muslim bi Sharḥ al-Nawawi"; Beirut: Dār al-Fikr, 1995, 3:1/4 Na'um Shaqir. Tarikh al-Sudan. Beirut: Dar al-Jil, 1981, 1/9

(an-)Nawawi; "Sharh Sahih Muslim"; No. 520

(al-)Nawawī, Yahya b. Sharaf; "Sahīh Muslim bi Sharh al-Nawawi"; Beirut: Dār al-Fikr, 1995, 3:1/4

(an-)Ninawi; "Sharh an-Ninawi ala Muslim"; No. 2472

Osada, Masako; "Sanctions and Honorary Whites: Diplomatic Policies and Economic Realities In Relations Between Japan and South Africa"; (Praeger,2002)

Park, Dr. Yoon Jung... Afro-Hispanic Review; "White, Honorary White, or Non-White: Apartheid Era Constructions of Chinese, (Univ of Johannesburg), Spring 2008

Political Testament of Adolf Hitler, The; Note #5, (February–April 1945)

Pooya, Mirza Mahdi Ayatullah; "Essence of the Holy Quran: The Eternal Light"; (Imam Sahab-uz-Zaman Association, 1990)

Qur'an; 16:36

Qur'an; 40:78

Qur'an 28:4

Qur'an 79:24

Qur'an; 2:115

Qur'an; 20:55

(ar-)Radi, Ash-Sharif; "Khasa'is Amir al-Mu'minin Ali bin Abi Talib"; Page 88

(as-)San'ani, Abd ar-Razzaq; "Al-Musannaf"; No. 10086

(al-)Suyuti, 'Abd al-Rahman Jalal al-Din; "Tarikh al-Khulafa"; Cairo: Dar al-Fajr li al-Turath, 2004, Page 86

Imam Suyuti relates this hadith from Sa'id b. Mansur via Sa'id b. al-Musayyab and Ibn Abi Layla.

"Tahdhib al-Tahdhib"; Volume 4 No. 14

Time; "South Africa: Honorary Whites"; 19 January 1962

(at-)Tirmidhi; "Sunan at-Tirmidhi"; No. 3718

World Health Organisation; "Preventing Disease through Healthy Environments: Mercury in Skin Lightening Products."; 2011 report. (http://www.who.int/ipcs/assessment/public_health/ mercury_flyer.pdf). See also Adow, Mohammed. "Nigeria's Skin Whitening Obsession: Nigeria has the world's highest percentage of women using skin lightening agents in the quest for "beauty."" Al-Jazeera: 6 April 2013. (http://www.aljazeera.com/indepth/features/2013/04/20134514845907984.html)

(al-)Waqidi; "Futuh as-Sham"; Volume 1, Page 156

(al-)Yahsubī, Qāḍī ʿAyyāḍ Abū al-Faḍl; "Al-Shifā bi Taʿrīf Ḥuqūq al-Muṣṭafā"; Beirut: Dār al-Kutub al-ʿIlmiya, 2000, Page 130-183.

Az-Zamakhshari; "Rabi'a al-Abrar wa Fusus al-Akhbar fi al-Muhadarat"; Juz 1, Page 191

40196743R00067

Made in the USA
Middletown, DE
06 February 2017